We the People...

do ordain and establish this
Constitution for the United States of America

A Secondary Level Student Text

Prepared for the

**National Bicentennial Competition on the
Constitution and Bill of Rights**

Directed by the
Center for Civic Education

Cosponsored by the
**Commission on the Bicentennial of the
United States Constitution**

Center for Civic Education 5146 Douglas Fir Road ▪ Calabasas, Ca 91302 ▪ 818/340-9320

The Center for Civic Education is a California nonprofit educational corporation established by and affiliated with the State Bar of California.

This text was developed with the support of the Commission on the Bicentennial of the United States Constitution, United States Department of Education, and the Office of Juvenile Justice and Deliquency Prevention of the United States Department of Justice.

ISBN 89818-126-7

Acknowledgements

The following staff, consultants, and members of the Board of Directors of the Center for Civic Education have contributed to the development of this text.

Editorial Directors
Charles N. Quigley
Duane E. Smith
Margaret S. Branson

Editorial Associates
Jane G. Sure
Judith A. Matz
Kenneth Rodriguez

Production Director
Kerin Martin

Consulting Associates
Charles F. Bahmueller
Howard Gilman
Jack N. Hoar
Douglas S. Hobbs
William Landau
Alita Letwin
Howard Safier
Mary Jane Turner

Artwork and Graphics
Richard Stein

Production Assistants
Lise Borja
Roslyn Danberg
Anne Drooker
Pat Mathwig
Miq Millman
Jan Ruyle

Photo Research
Rebecca Hirsh

This text is the result of a field testing program involving over 250 educators and 11,000 students in 28 areas of the nation. The comments and suggestions of these colleagues and students have been invaluable in the revision and improvement of this edition of the text. The Center is grateful for the assistance of all of those who have contributed their criticisms and suggestions.

The Center is also grateful for the many helpful comments and suggestions that have been received from the following persons who have reviewed the manuscript in its various developmental stages. The Center has attempted to be responsive to all of the many valuable suggestions for improvement in the text. However, the final product is the responsibility of the Center and does not necessarily reflect the views of those who have contributed their thoughts and ideas.

William G. Baker, Governor's Task Force on Citizenship Education, Indiana
Jack Barlow, Assistant Director for Educational Programs, Commission on the Bicentennial of the United States Constitution
Michael Les Benedict, Professor, Department of History, Ohio State University
Gayle Binion, Executive Director, American Civil Liberties Union of Southern California
Vincent M. Bonventre, Judicial Fellow, Federal Judicial Center
Margaret Branson, Director of Curricular Services, Kern County Superintendent of Schools Office, Bakersfield, California
R. Freeman Butts, Senior Fellow, Kettering Foundation
Mark Cannon, Staff Director, Commission on the Bicentennial of the United States Constitution

Erwin Chemerinsky, Professor, The Law Center, University of Southern California
William Cohen, Professor, School of Law, Stanford University
Jerry Combee, Dean, School of Business and Government, Liberty University
J. Peter Euben, Professor, Politics and Classics, University of California, Santa Cruz
Anne Fickling, Research Assistant to Director for Educational Programs, Commission on the Bicentennial of the United States Constitution
James H. Kettner, Professor, Department of History, University of California, Berkeley
Frances Kolb, Staff Associate, The Network Inc., Andover, Massachusetts
Joseph McElligott, Director, Division of Education, California Catholic Conference

Sheilah Mann, Director, Project '87 of the American Political Science Association and the American Historical Association
Gary B. Nash, Professor, Department of History, University of California, Los Angeles
Jewel L. Prestage, Dean, School of Public Policy and Urban Affairs, Southern University
Jack N. Rakove, Professor, Department of History, Stanford University
Philippa Strum, Professor, Department of Political Science, Brooklyn College of The City University of New York
Albion M. Urdank, Professor, Department of History, University of California, Los Angeles
Jonathan D. Varat, Professor, School of Law, University of California, Los Angeles
Richard Vetterli, Professor, Department of Political Science, Brigham Young University

Table of Contents

Unit Four: Establishment of the Government

Unit Five: Fundamental Rights

Unit Six: Responsibilities of the Citizen

Reference Section

Introduction

by

Warren E. Burger, Chairman

Commission on the Bicentennial of the United States Constitution

Chief Justice of the United States, 1969-1986

The years 1987 to 1991 mark the 200th anniversary of the writing, ratification, and implementation of the basic documents of American democracy, the Constitution and the Bill of Rights. Our Constitution has stood the tests and stresses of time, wars, and change. Although it was not perfect, as Benjamin Franklin and many others recognized, it has lasted because it was carefully crafted by men who understood the importance of a system of government sufficiently strong to meet the challenges of the day, yet sufficiently flexible to accommodate and adapt to new political, economic, and social conditions.

Many Americans have but a slight understanding of the Constitution, the Bill of Rights, and the later amendments to which we pledge our allegiance. The lessons in this book are designed to give you, the next generation of American citizens, an understanding of the background, creation, and subsequent history of the unique system of government brought into being by our Constitution. At the same time, it will help you understand the principles and ideals that underlie and give meaning to the Constitution, a system of government by those governed.

Unit One: Political Philosophy

Delegates to the Philadelphia Convention, 1787

Purpose of Unit One

Our Constitution establishes the form of government we have today. It was created in Philadelphia during the summer of 1787 by a group of 55 delegates from the new states that had recently gained their freedom from British rule. These men brought with them a considerable knowledge of government. They had gained this knowledge by studying the writings of political philosophers and historians who had written about government over the past two thousand years. They had also had experience with government themselves. They had, to a large extent, governed themselves even before the Revolution. They had also had the experience of governing the newly independent states. They used this knowledge and experience when they wrote the Constitution. An understanding of what they had learned will help you understand why they wrote the Constitution as they did and why we have the kind of government we have today. It will also help you understand the most important principles and values of our government.

This unit will provide you with an overview of some of the most important ideas from political philosophy that influenced the writing of our Constitution and Bill of Rights. In the next unit you will learn about some of the most important historical events, as well as the experiences of the Founders with government, that influenced the creation of our Constitution.

Throughout this text we will use the word Founders to refer to all of the men and women who lived in America throughout the colonial period who were influential in creating our government. We will use the word Framers to refer to those delegates who met in Philadelphia to write our Constitution. For example, John Adams, Mercy Otis Warren, Thomas Paine, Patrick Henry, and Thomas Jefferson were Founders, but not Framers, because they did not attend the Philadelphia Convention.

It is particularly important to understand the ideas in this unit because they provide a frame of reference for understanding the rest of the lessons in this text.

The most important ideas and terms used in each lesson throughout the text are listed at the beginning of the lesson. These ideas and terms are defined in the lesson itself or in the glossary at the end of the text.

What would life be like in a "state of nature"?

Purpose of Lesson 1

The first and second lessons in this unit will introduce you to some of the basic ideas of the natural rights philosophy which were of great importance in the development of our government. The most important ideas contained in Lesson 1 are listed below.

When you finish this lesson, you should be able to explain these ideas, their place in the natural rights philosophy, the source of the ideas, and how they influenced the kind of government the Founders created.

    political philosophy
    state of nature
    law of nature
    consent
    natural rights philosophy
    human nature

John Locke, English political philosopher, 1632-1704

The natural rights philosophy

We hold these Truths to be self-evident, that all Men are created equal, that they are endowed by their Creator with certain unalienable Rights, that among these are Life, Liberty, and the Pursuit of Happiness--That to secure these Rights, Governments are instituted among Men, deriving their just Powers from the Consent of the Governed, that whenever any Form of Government becomes destructive of these Ends, it is the Right of the People to alter or to abolish it, and to institute new Government... (Declaration of Independence, *1776*)

This excerpt from the Declaration of Independence includes some of the most important philosophical ideas underlying our form of government. They are ideas that had been accepted by almost everyone in the American colonies long before the Revolutionary War. They had been preached in churches, written in pamphlets, and debated in public and private. These basic ideas had been developed and refined by political philosophers such as the Englishman John Locke (1632-1704) and by many others in Europe and in the colonies. Of these philosophers, John Locke was the most important influence on the thinking of the Founders at the time of the Revolution. The political philosophy Locke wrote about is often called the natural rights philosophy.

The natural rights philosophy is based on imagining what life would be like if there were no government. Locke and others called this imaginary situation a state of nature. Whether or not such a state ever existed, thinking about what life would be like if there were no government was very useful to philosophers such as Locke in answering the following questions.

1. What is human nature, that is, what traits of personality and character, if any, do all people have in common? For example, are all people basically selfish or do they tend to care for the welfare of others?

2. What should be the purpose of government?

3. How do the people running a government get the right to govern?

4. How should a government be organized?

5. What kinds of governments should be respected and supported?

6. What kinds of governments should be resisted and fought?

John Locke's answers to these questions were the answers accepted by most of the Founders. They used these ideas to explain and justify their declaration of independence from Great Britain. They also used these ideas in writing the various state constitutions after the Revolutionary War and later in writing the Constitution of the United States.

Problem solving

It's your turn to think like a philosopher

In order to understand the natural rights philosophy, it is helpful to try to answer the questions it deals with. Some of the most important of these questions are included in the following exercise. You may not all agree on your answers to these questions.

It is important to know that you are not alone. At various times in history, people have had very different views on these matters.

Imagine that all of the students in your school were transported to a place where there were enough natural resources for you to live on, but where no one had lived before. When you arrived, you had no means of communicating with people in other parts of the world. On the basis of this situation, answer the following questions, discuss your answers, and then compare your answers with those of John Locke which follow.

1. Would there be any government or laws to control how you lived, what rights or freedoms you exercised, or what property you had? Why?

2. Would anyone have the right to govern you? Would you have the right to govern anyone else? Why?

3. Would you have any rights? What would they be? Would it make any difference if you were a man or a woman?

4. What might people who were stronger than others try to do? Why?

5. What might the weaker people try to do? Why?

6. What might life be like for everyone?

Compare your answers with John Locke's

Your answers to the above questions may be similar to the following answers developed by John Locke or they may differ. In this lesson, however, we are focusing on understanding Locke's answers because they were widely shared by Americans living during the 1700s and played a very important role in the development of our government.

1. It is clear that Locke believed that there were laws in a state of nature. He said, "The state of nature has a law of nature to govern it which obliges every one . . no one ought to harm another in his life, health, liberty, or possessions . . ." These laws were "the Laws of Nature and of Nature's God" as Thomas Jefferson called them in the Declaration of Independence.

However, the problem in the state of nature would be that you and others would probably disagree on what the "laws of nature" are and there would be no one with the right to help you settle your disagreements. This is because there would be no government to say what the law was or to enforce it.

According to Locke, there wouldn't be any government because a government can't exist until it has been created. And a legitimate or just government cannot exist until the people have given their consent to be ruled by it. Thomas Jefferson included this idea in the Declaration when he wrote that

"Governments are instituted among men, deriving their just powers from the consent of the governed; . . ."

2. No one would have the right to govern you, nor would you have the right to govern anyone else. According to Locke, the only way anyone gets the right to govern anyone is if the person to be governed gives his or her <u>consent</u>. If people haven't consented to the creation of a government, there is no government.

3. You would have the right to life, liberty, and property. This means you would have the right to defend these rights if other people threatened to take them away. These were called <u>natural rights</u>. We now call them fundamental, basic, or human rights.

4. Locke believed that people are basically reasonable and sociable, but that they are also self-interested. Since the only security people would have for the protection of their natural rights would be their own strength or cunning, people who were stronger or more able would often try to take away the life, liberty, or property of the weak.

5. Weaker people might try to protect themselves by joining against the strong.

6. Because there would be no laws that everybody agreed upon and no government to enforce them, everybody's rights would be very insecure.

The problems of a state of nature

John Locke and most Americans in the eighteenth century thought that people are equal in their rights to life, liberty, and property. They have these <u>natural rights</u> just because they are human beings. This means that in a state of nature, no one would have the right to interfere with your life or property or your freedom to do as you wished. However, Locke also believed that in that kind of situation, because of human nature, there would always be people who would try to violate your rights. Since there would not be any government, you and others would have to defend your rights against those who might want to take them away. The result would be that in the state of nature, your rights would be insecure and you would be in constant danger of losing them.

For Locke and those who shared his ideas, the great problem was to find a way to protect our natural rights so that we can live at peace with one another and enjoy them.

Reviewing and using the lesson

1. The Declaration of Independence contains some of the most important ideas of the American system of government. These are often called the natural rights philosophy. Briefly describe some of the major points of this philosophy.

2. According to Locke, what is the purpose of government?

3. It has been said that since people are not equal in their intelligence and character, it is unjust for all to have the same rights. Do you agree? Why?

4. Imagine yourself living in a community where all governmental authority has broken down. Violent lawlessness is widespread. Do you think <u>any</u> government is better than none? Why?

5. How might your ideas about what human beings are "really like" influence your ideas about what type of government is best?

4

Why have a government?

Purpose of Lesson 2

This lesson introduces several more basic ideas that complete your study of the natural rights philosophy. Be prepared to explain the following ideas and their relevance to our government when you complete the lesson.

social contract
compact or covenant
purposes of government
right to revolution

The insecurity of life in a state of nature

In the last lesson we asked you to imagine that you lived in a place where there was no government. Suppose that in such a situation you believe that everyone has natural rights to life, liberty, and property. You know that these rights are in danger because people will not always respect the rights of others. While there is a law of nature telling you how to behave, people disagree about what that law says. Some will interpret it according to their own needs and interests. Since there is no government, there is no one to make laws that you can understand and follow and no one to enforce them. As a result, you and everyone else must defend your rights, and you live in a situation in which they may be taken from you. How should you solve this problem?

John Locke's solution--the social contract

Locke said that the best way to solve the problem of the state of nature is for you to give up the natural freedom you would have in order to gain protection for your rights. To gain this protection, he believed you should agree with others to create and live under a government and give it the power to make laws and to enforce them. This kind of an agreement is called the social contract. Sometimes it is called the social compact, as in the "Mayflower Compact." Others have called it a covenant.

As in all contracts, in order to get something, you must give something in return. In the social contract, everyone promises to give up the absolute right to do anything he or she has the right to do in a state of nature. In return, everyone receives the security that can be provided by a government. Each person consents to obey the limits placed upon him or her by the laws created by the government. Everyone gains the peace of knowing that his or her rights to life, liberty, and property are protected.

Problem solving
Answering philosophical questions

Suppose, then, that you and everyone else in your imaginary state of nature do agree to live under a government. There are several more questions of the natural rights philosophers that you must answer in deciding what kind of government to create. Answer the following questions, discuss your answers, and then compare them with those of John Locke.

1. What do you think the main purpose of government should be?

2. How should government get the authority or right to make laws telling people what they can and can't do?

3. What should the people have the right to do if their government does not serve the purposes for which they created it? Why should they have this right?

Compare your answers with John Locke's

1. Locke and other natural rights philosophers said that the purpose of government is to protect your natural rights. In the Declaration of Independence, Thomas Jefferson argued that the protection of rights is the main purpose of government. So did the Framers, as we can see by reading the Preamble to the Constitution. Read it and see where it contains this idea. What other purposes of government does the Preamble mention?

We, the People of the United States, in order to form a more perfect union, establish justice, insure domestic tranquility, provide for the common defence, promote the general welfare, and secure the blessings of liberty to ourselves and our posterity, do ordain and establish this Constitution for the United States of America. (Preamble to the Constitution of the United States, 1787)

One purpose of government, according to the Preamble, is not only to give us laws to protect our rights so we can live together peacefully and enjoy security, but it is also to "promote the general welfare." You will learn more about this added purpose and what it means in the next lesson.

2. Both the Declaration of Independence and the Preamble contain another basic idea about government. This idea is that government gets its right to govern from the consent of the governed. Its powers are delegated to it by the people.

Library of Congress

Signing the Mayflower compact, 1620

6

3. Locke believed that since the people give the power to the government, they have the right to take it away if the government is not serving the purposes for which it was established. They can then create a new government. Locke and the Founders argued that if a government fails to protect the people's rights, the people have a right to revolution.

But who is to judge if the government has failed? Locke and the Founders said that the people have the right to make that decision. This position is contained in the following words from the Declaration of Independence, ". . . that whenever any Form of Government becomes destructive of these Ends, it is the Right of the People to alter or to abolish it, and to institute new Government, . . ."

What kind of government is most likely to protect the basic rights of the people?

Suppose you are not satisfied with living in a state of nature. You and others agree to a social contract and the creation of a government. Next, you must decide what kind of government you want and then establish it. Locke, Jefferson, and almost all of the ancient and medieval philosophers knew that this is not an easy task. Throughout history governments have deprived people of their rights more often than they have protected them. Your problem is to design and establish the kind of government that will do what you want it to do, that is, protect your rights. That means providing equal protection for the rights of everyone.

The remaining lessons in this unit will help you understand some of the basic ideas the Framers used in creating the kind of government they thought would be best to protect their rights and promote the general welfare.

Reviewing and using the lesson

1. What is the problem of the state of nature? What was John Locke's solution?

2. According to the Declaration of Independence and the Preamble to the Constitution, where do governments get their authority to rule?

3. According to Locke and the Founders, under what circumstances do the people have the right to alter or abolish their government?

4. List at least three examples of recent actions taken by your local, state, or federal government which affect your life, liberty, or property. (For example, some states have passed laws prohibiting smoking in public places.)

5. Locke believed that people had equal rights in a state of nature--no person had any right to tell others what to do. What kind of government do you think would be associated with the opposite belief--that some people are more capable of ruling your life than you are?

6. How could you organize a government so it would be fairly easy to remove and replace members of the government you thought were not doing a good job?

7. How might members of government be removed in a nation if there were no agreed-upon or peaceful means of removing them? What might this situation lead to? Give a contemporary example.

8. In what ways, if any, do you think many people's definitions of basic rights today might differ from that of Locke and Jefferson? Explain your answer.

What is republican government?

A Roman leader, Cincinnatus, demonstrates civic virtue by leaving his plow to defend the Republic

Library of Congress

Purpose of Lesson 3

Lesson 2 introduced the question, "What kind of government is best?" This lesson will introduce you to some of the basic ideas the Founders used in answering this question and why they chose the answers they did. It includes an introduction to the idea of <u>republicanism</u> which was of great importance in the development of our government.

When you finish this lesson, you should be able to explain the ideas and terms listed below, how they influenced the Founders, and their importance to our government.

> **civic virtue**
> **common welfare/common good**
> **republican government**
> **purpose of republican government**
> **balanced powers**
> **mixed constitution**
> **Judeo-Christian heritage**
> **corrupt government**
> **representative democracy**

The Roman Republic

As you have learned, the Founders had read the writings of the natural rights philosophers and had adopted many of their ideas about government. They had also studied and been influenced by philosophers who had written about ancient government. They were particularly interested in what they had read about the government of the ancient Roman Republic which had lasted for nearly 500 years between 509 B.C. and 27 B.C. But why were they so impressed by a government that had existed two thousand years earlier?

The historical accounts of ancient Rome during the greatest days of the Roman Republic described the Roman people as having <u>civic virtue</u>. By this the historians meant that the Roman people were hard-working, simple in their ways of life, honest, and patriotic. Above all, the people loved justice and liberty. Loving their country more than themselves, the common people and the aristocracy shared political powers. The virtuous Romans governed themselves without a king.

As a result, they had a government that provided justice and protected their liberty. It was a government that promoted the common good or the common welfare. This kind of government was called republican government. The main purpose of republican government was to promote the common welfare. This is what made it superior to most other kinds of government which only promoted the welfare of one person, such as a tyrant, or of a particular class of people such as the rich or the poor.

Whether or not the people and government of the Roman Republic were as admirable as they were described by some historians, the accounts of their virtues greatly influenced the Founders.

The need for civic virtue

The lesson the Founders learned from the example of the Roman Republic was that in order to have a government that protected their rights and promoted the common welfare, the citizens must possess civic virtue. This meant that citizens must love their country, be honest, be hard-working, and live a modest way of life. These qualities of character needed to be encouraged and developed by the family, by religion, by education, and finally, by the performance of the duties of citizenship.

Library of Congress
Montesquieu, French political philosopher, 1689 - 1755

How should a government be organized so it will promote the common welfare?

In addition to the example of the ancient Roman Republic, the Founders also learned about republican government from writers of their own time. One of the most important of these was Montesquieu (1689-1755), a French writer who was widely admired by Americans. He was often called "the celebrated Montesquieu," and many of the Founders considered him to be the most important writer on republican government.

Balanced powers

Montesquieu believed that the English system of government was the best example of how a republican government should be organized. He argued that in the English system, the powers of government were divided and balanced among the King and two houses of Parliament--a House of Lords and a House of Commons. The King represented the interests of royalty. The House of Lords represented the interests of the nobility. The House of Commons represented the interests of the common people.

A "mixed constitution"

Like the ancient philosophers Aristotle and Cicero, Montesquieu believed that a system which divided and balanced the power of government among the different classes of society, as was done in Great Britain, was the best way to be sure that the government would not be dominated by a single social class. He called this type of government a mixed constitution because it combined the three basic types of government, monarchy, aristocracy, and democracy, into one. Since all classes shared power, this kind of government was the best for serving the common welfare.

What is the importance of civic virtue to republican government?

Remember that one of the things that impressed Americans about the Roman Republic was the virtue of its citizens. Many of the supporters of republican government believed that it could only succeed if the citizens were virtuous. Montesquieu agreed. He wrote that the virtue of the good citizen of a republic is really a very simple thing. It meant that citizens must constantly prefer the common welfare to their own private interests. This, the Founders thought, was the virtue of the citizens of ancient Rome.

The Founders believed most Americans had the same virtue as the citizens of Rome. They believed this virtue came from the Americans' Judeo-Christian heritage. Citizens who had a sincere interest in the common welfare would behave as good republican citizens should.

What kind of society is necessary for a republican government?

Montesquieu had written, and many Founders agreed, that people would only be willing to promote the common welfare instead of their own interests if none of them were too rich or too poor. For this reason, they thought that people of the middle class were most likely to possess civic virtue. People who were very wealthy or very poor would be more likely to promote their own interests at the expense of the common welfare. When a government serves such special interests at the expense of the common welfare, it is said to be <u>corrupt</u>. The Founders believed that great wealth or poverty in a society were the most likely sources of corruption.

Why is a small nation necessary for republican government?

Montesquieu also said that since promoting the common welfare is the main purpose of republican government, this type of government is only possible in small nations. If you tried to have a republican form of government in a large and diverse nation, it would be very difficult for the people to agree about what was best for their common welfare.

What did republican government mean to the Founders?

Some of the basic ideas of republican government were being put into practice by the English at the time the colonies were being settled in America. The first lesson in the next unit deals with the history of the English government. It provides an important background for understanding the government created by the colonists in America who rebelled against their mother country. But first, we should look at how the ideas of republicanism were developed in America.

We have learned that the Founders believed that the purpose of government should be to protect each individual's natural rights. They also believed that republican government was the best solution to the problem raised by Lesson 2, that is, "What kind of government is most likely to protect the basic rights of the people?"

What is the common welfare?

Republican government promotes the common welfare. But what is the common welfare? This is not always an easy question to answer. Different people have had and will continue to have very different ideas about what the common welfare is. The Founders, however, believed that a government that promotes the common welfare is one that protects each individual's natural rights.

The Founders also believed that a republican form of government was the only kind that they should have and they believed that Americans had the civic virtue necessary to make a republic work. However, there were still some problems with republicanism that needed to be worked out.

James Madison, 1751 - 1836

James Madison refines the idea of republicanism

James Madison was one of the most important of the Founders responsible for creating our Constitution. He said that there was an important difference between a republic and a democracy. He defined a democracy as a small community or nation with a small number of citizens who meet from time to time to do the tasks of government themselves. The Greek city-states and the New England towns were examples of democracies as Madison defined them.

Madison defined a republic as a country in which laws are made and administered by representatives elected by the people. In a republic, all of the powers of the government are given to it by the people. The representatives who run it have their jobs for a limited amount of time or as long as they behave properly. Madison also insisted that members of government should be elected by a large number of the people in the society and not by a small number or a specially favored group. If that happened, the government would only serve the interests of a small group instead of the common welfare.

A republican government is a representative democracy

According to Madison, then, a republican government is a representative democracy. It gets its authority, its right to govern, from the people it governs. The citizens of the republic must possess the civic virtue to elect people of wisdom and character to represent them in the government.

The need for a constitution

There is, however, one additional part of a republican government the Founders thought was necessary, a written constitution. They had a firm belief in the superiority of constitutional government, or constitutionalism. A good constitution, they believed, was one of the most important ways to protect a republican government, which in turn was the only way to protect their natural rights.

As we shall see, the Founders' belief in natural rights, republicanism, and constitutionalism greatly influenced their creation of our Constitution. But, before we study our Constitution, we must learn in the next lesson what constitutional government is and how it is different from other kinds of government.

Reviewing and using the lesson

1. What is the purpose of republican government? What characteristics must the people have to maintain such governments?

2. What features of the British government of his day led Montesquieu to think that it was the best way to maintain a republican government?

3. Give two characteristics of a people that Montesquieu and the Founders believed necessary for republican government.

4. How did Madison distinguish between a "democracy" and a "republic"?

5. A republican government may aim to (a) protect the individual's rights and (b) promote the common welfare. Give examples from history and your own experience in which these two goals conflict with each other.

What is constitutional government?

Purpose of Lesson 4

This lesson introduces two main ideas. They are the ideas of (a) <u>constitution</u> and (b) <u>constitutional government</u>. Since these ideas are so important in understanding governments and the development of our own constitutional government, we will define them as clearly as possible.

When you finish the lesson, you should be able to explain what a constitution is, what a constitutional government is, and some of the essential differences between constitutional governments and autocratic or dictatorial governments. You should also be able to explain the other basic ideas that are listed below.

> **constitution**
> **written and unwritten constitutions**
> **constitutional government**
> **autocratic or dictatorial government**
> **limited government**
> **higher law**
> **private domain**

THE ILLUSTRATED NEWS, NEW YORK PUBLIC LIBRARY

Abraham Lincoln is inaugurated in March, 1861, on the eve of the Civil War

Defining "constitution"

A <u>constitution</u> is a set of fundamental customs, traditions, rules, and laws that sets forth the basic way a government is organized and operated. Most constitutions are in writing, some are partly written and partly unwritten, and some are not written at all.

If you study the constitution of a government, you will often be able to answer the following questions about the relationship between the government and its citizens.

<u>Government</u>

- What are the purposes of the government?

- How is the government organized?

- How is the government supposed to go about doing its business?

<u>Citizens</u>

- Who is considered to be a citizen?

- Are the citizens supposed to have any power or control over their government? If so, how is it to be exercised?

- What rights and responsibilities, if any, are the citizens supposed to have?

According to this definition of a constitution, <u>every</u> nation has a constitution. Good governments and bad governments have constitutions. Some of the worst governments have constitutions that include lists of the basic rights of their citizens. A list of rights does not mean that the citizens actually have those rights.

Having a constitution does not mean that a nation has a <u>constitutional government</u>. If, for example, a constitution provides for the <u>unlimited</u> exercise of political power--by one, few, or even many--it would not be the basis of a constitutional government. If a constitution says that the power of the government is to be limited, but it <u>does not</u> include ways to enforce those limitations, it also is not the basis of a constitutional government.

The dictatorial government led by Adolf Hitler that ruled Germany from 1933 - 1945 exercised unlimited power

Defining "constitutional government"

A constitutional government is best understood by comparing it with an autocratic or dictatorial government.

In an <u>autocratic or dictatorial government</u>, whether ruled by one person or many, power is <u>unlimited</u>. The person or persons who ultimately control the government can do whatever they want to do with the nation's citizens and resources.

In a <u>constitutional government</u>, the powers of the person or group controlling the government are <u>limited</u> by a set of laws and/or established customs called a <u>constitution</u> which they <u>must</u> and <u>do</u> obey.

As you have learned, all governments have constitutions that set forth the ways they are organized and operated. But only in a constitutional government is the constitution considered to be a form of <u>higher law</u> that must be obeyed by the persons running the government.

The characteristics of the higher law

In a constitutional government, the constitution or higher law has the following characteristics.

- It sets forth the basic rights of citizens to life, liberty, and property.

- It establishes the responsibility of the government to protect those rights.

- It establishes limitations on how those in government may use their powers with regard to (a) citizens' rights and responsibilities, (b) the distribution of resources, and (c) the control of conflict.

- It establishes the principle of a private domain--which means that there are areas of citizens' lives that are no business of the government and in which the government cannot interfere.

- It can only be changed with the widespread consent of the citizens, and according to established and well-known procedures.

What kinds of governments may be constitutional governments?

It is possible in theory to have a constitutional government that is ruled by one person or a small group of people, so long as the rulers obey the limitations on their powers placed upon them by the "higher law" of the constitution.

But history has shown that a problem often arises when a constitutional government is ruled by one person or a small group of people. If all of the power is

13

given to a select few, it is difficult to make sure that they will obey the limitations placed upon them by the constitution. The rulers in such a nation would control its armed forces and law-enforcement agencies. What group of citizens would have the power to force the rulers to obey the constitution? Both history and contemporary events show us that the misuse of governmental power can threaten and even destroy the lives, liberty, and property of citizens.

Problem solving

The Founders' fear of the abuse of power

Given their knowledge of history and their experiences with the British government, it is not surprising that the Founders greatly feared the possible abuse of the powers of government. Read, for example, the following selections from the writings of some of the most prominent Founders. Then discuss your answers to the questions that follow the selections.

Give all power to the many, they will oppress the few. Give all power to the few, they will oppress the many. (Alexander Hamilton, American statesman, 1787.)

There are two passions which have a powerful influence on the affairs of men. These are ambition and avarice; the love of power and the love of money. (Benjamin Franklin, American statesman and philosopher, 1787.)

From the nature of man, we may be sure that those who have power in their hands. . . will always, when they can . . . increase it. (George Mason, American statesman, 1787.)

1. Explain the view of human nature that is expressed in the above quotations by several of the Founders.

2. If you held the view of human nature expressed above, what kind of safeguards would you include in your government to prevent the abuse of its powers?

Reviewing and using the lesson

1. What is a constitution? What can you learn of a nation's government by studying its constitution?

2. All governments have constitutions. Only some of these governments are constitutional governments. Explain the essential differences between constitutional governments and autocratic or dictatorial governments.

3. What characteristics does the "higher law" of a constitutional government have?

4. Review the basic ideas listed at the beginning of this lesson and be sure you can explain each of them.

How can constitutional governments be organized to prevent the abuse of power?

Purpose of Lesson 5

You learned in the last lesson of the fear of the Founders that the powers of government might be abused at the expense of the people. This fear was not unreasonable given their knowledge of history and their beliefs about human nature. This final lesson of Unit One deals with some of the ideas used by the Framers to organize our government so it would be difficult to abuse its powers.

After studying the lesson, you should be able to explain the following ideas and to identify examples of their use in our government.

separation of powers
checks and balances
legislative branch
executive branch
judicial branch
veto

Organizing a constitutional government

A study of constitutional governments will show that their powers are usually distributed among several different groups. This distribution of power makes it less likely that any one group will be able to abuse or misuse its powers. Also, it is less likely that any group will gain so much power that it can ignore the limitations placed upon it by the constitution. To prevent the abuse of the powers of our government, the Framers provided for the separation of its powers and a system of checks and balances.

Separation of powers

In modern constitutional systems, powers are commonly divided among three branches of government.

- The legislative branch is responsible for making laws.

- The administrative or executive branch is responsible for carrying out and enforcing laws.

- The judicial branch is responsible for managing conflicts over the interpretation, application, and enforcement of laws.

Checks and balances

The phrase checks and balances means that the powers given to the different branches of government are distributed or "balanced" so that no branch has so much power that it can completely dominate the others. Although each branch of the government has its own special powers, many of these powers are "checked" because they are shared with the other groups.

For instance, in the United States, the power to make laws is given to the legislative branch of government. This legislative power is divided between the House of Representatives and the Senate, which check each other. In addition, the executive and judicial branches have been given ways to check and control this power of the legislature. For example,

- the President can check the power of Congress by vetoing its laws, and

- the Supreme Court can check the power of Congress by declaring its laws to be in violation of the Constitution and, therefore, invalid.

In much the same way, the powers of the President and Supreme Court are checked by the other branches. You will learn more about this system in later lessons.

The complexity of constitutional government

The complicated ways in which constitutional governments are organized often mean that it takes them a long time to get things done. In fact, it is almost impossible to get something done if there are powerful conflicting interests involved. It may seem strange, but this "inefficiency" was seen by the Framers as an advantage. Many people think that these difficulties make it more likely that when a decision is finally made, it will be a good one.

Reviewing and using the lesson

1. What powers of government are usually separated in modern constitutional governments? Why?

2. To which branches of our government are the powers you have identified given?

3. In constitutional governments, a separate branch is often "checked" or "balanced" by the other branches. Why? Give examples of these "checks and balances."

4. The separation and sharing of powers may make quick responses to common problems unlikely. Why do you think the Framers chose these arrangements over other, possibly more efficient, ways of organizing a government? Do you agree with them? Why?

16

Unit Two: History and Experience

King John signing the Magna Carta, 1215

Purpose of Unit Two

In the first unit of this text, you have studied some of the basic ideas of the <u>natural rights philosophy</u>, <u>republicanism</u>, and <u>constitutional government</u> which influenced the thinking of the Framers. However, these were not the only influences upon their thinking. Many of them had studied the history of government in Western civilization. Most of them had had personal experience in government before and after the Revolution. This unit will provide you with an overview of some of the most important historical events and experiences which influenced the writing of our Constitution.

What basic ideas of constitutional government were found in the government of England?

Purpose of Lesson 6

This lesson describes the evolution of constitutional government in England. As you read the lesson, look carefully to see how the basic ideas about government that you have studied were developed in English history.

When you complete this lesson, you should be able to explain some of the most important events in the development of English constitutional government. You should also be able to explain the basic ideas and terms introduced in the lesson which are listed below.

> **source of authority**
> **divine right of kings**
> **subject**
> **feudal government**
> **royalty**
> **nobility**
> **commons**
> **balance of power**
> **balanced constitution**
> **Magna Carta**

The beginnings of English government

For the first thousand or so years after the birth of Christ, England was divided among a number of tribes, each ruled by its own leader or king. These early kings were <u>selected</u> by councils of advisers because they were the strongest and most powerful members of their tribes. For many years these tribes were at war with each other. Eventually all of the tribes of England became united under one king.

After England became a Christian country, the kings claimed that the <u>source of their authority</u> was the "will of God," an idea that became known as the <u>divine right of kings</u>.

Under this early kind of English <u>monarchy,</u> all of the people were <u>subject</u> to the king's rule--which is why they were called his "subjects." The king exercised his control with the help of a council of trusted advisers.

England was a large nation for one person to rule in those times, since there were no quick and efficient means of communication or travel. Most kings simply preferred to let people in local areas control themselves according to customs that had developed over the years.

Feudal government

A major change in the way England was ruled took place on October 14, 1066, when William the Conqueror, the leader of the Normans, completed his invasion of England by defeating King Harold in the Battle of Hastings. As a result, a new <u>feudal</u> system of government was imposed on the people of England. The feudal government had the following characteristics.

- All of the people of the nation were classified as belonging to one of three groups, called "orders." These were (a) <u>royalty</u>, which included the king and queen and their family; (b) the <u>nobility</u>, which included the "lords" and "ladies" who were the major followers of the

18

king or queen and who held titles such as earl or baron; and (c) the commons or "common people," made up of such different groups as knights, merchants, and peasants. At that time the peasants were called "serfs" because they were not free and were forced to work on the land.

- All of the territory of England was considered to belong to the king or queen. Everyone living in the kingdom was subject to the monarch's rule.

- Because there was so much territory to control, the king or queen gave some of the responsibility for governing the kingdom to the nobility. The nobles were allowed to control parts of the royal territory and the common people who lived upon it in exchange for military service. This convenient sharing of power by royalty with the nobility eventually led to the development of a different kind of government as you will soon learn.

Checking for understanding

1. What did early English kings claim was the source of their authority, that is, the source of their right to rule over their people? How does this source differ from the source of authority of the United States government?

2. What was the source of the nobles' authority to rule the people who were subject to them? How does this compare with the source of authority of a cabinet officer nominated by the President and confirmed by Congress?

3. How did the kings share their powers in the English feudal system?

The Magna Carta and the development of constitutional government

One of the most important changes in the government of England took place in 1215. This date is important in the development of constitutional government in England because in that year the power of the king became limited by a written document called the Magna Carta.

By this time, it had become traditional for the kings and queens of England to share some of their

powers with the nobility. In 1215, King John tried to take back some of the rights and powers the nobles had grown accustomed to having. The result was a war between the nobles and their king, a war that the nobles won.

The nobles then forced King John to sign the Magna Carta. It listed traditional rights of the nobles that the king could not take from them. The rights guaranteed included (a) the freedom of the church from the control of the king, (b) the independence of the courts of England, (c) the right of people who owned land to pass it on to their oldest son, (d) the right of people who owned land to a fair trial, (e) the right to travel, and (f) the freedom from unnecessary searches of their homes.

The early English customs and traditions and the Magna Carta protected certain basic rights. However, it is important to know that these rights did not apply to all of the people of England. Men who owned property were given far more rights than were women or children or others without property.

Checking for understanding

1. Identify and explain the basic ideas of constitutional government described above.

2. What were some of the basic rights included in the Magna Carta and what were their sources? Which of these rights do you think the Framers included in our Constitution?

The establishment of a balance of power among branches of government

Conflicts between the kings and their nobles continued after the signing of the Magna Carta. The Magna Carta showed how a written document or constitution could be used to place <u>limits</u> on governmental power. The next great change in the English government resulted in the <u>separation</u> of its powers.

In 1258, King Henry III and the nobles agreed to create a new council, called <u>Parliament</u>, to advise the king. During the next thirty years, Parliament became the branch of government that <u>represented</u> the most powerful orders or groups in the kingdom. The Parliament was made up of two houses: the <u>House of Lords</u> which represented the interests of the nobility, and the <u>House of Commons</u> which represented the "common people." However, at this time the "common people" were mainly people who owned large amounts of land but were not members of the nobility.

For hundreds of years royalty, nobility, and "commoners" struggled against each other for power. But no one group was able to control all of the power for very long. This struggle for the control of the government had a dramatic history. Consider, for example, the following events during the important years between 1621 and 1689--the time of the early settlement of the English colonies in America.

- 1621. Members of the House of Commons insisted on having the right to take part in making governmental decisions. King James I responded by disbanding Parliament the following year.

- 1628. Members of Parliament forced the king to sign the <u>Petition of Right</u>. The petition included the liberties Englishmen had won in the past and the customs they lived by and supported. Now the customs, traditions, and liberties of Englishmen were clearly set forth in an official <u>written</u> document agreed upon by Parliament and signed by the king.

- 1641. Parliament was powerful enough to pass a law denying the king the right to disband it without its <u>consent</u>.

- 1649. During the English Civil War, Parliament was powerful enough to put King Charles I on trial for treason and to have him executed!

- 1653-1658. Oliver Cromwell, an English general, took power and completely abolished the title and positions of the king and the House of Lords.

- 1660. The monarchy was restored and Charles II became king.

- 1688. King James II was forced to flee England because of his arbitrary methods of government. This ended the doctrine of the "divine right of kings."

- 1689. The <u>Toleration Act</u> increased the religious freedom of most people in England by allowing members of a variety of religious groups to practice their beliefs.

- 1689. Parliament created a <u>Bill of Rights</u>.

The English Bill of Rights

The English <u>Bill of Rights</u> of 1689 restored the <u>balance of power</u> between the king and Parliament that had been upset by King James II. Kings and queens were not allowed to (a) collect taxes without the <u>consent</u> of the Parliament, (b) interfere with the <u>right to free speech</u> and debate that went on in Parliament, (c) maintain an army in times of peace (since it might be used to take over the government), (d) require <u>excessive bail</u> or administer <u>cruel punishment</u>

for those accused or convicted of crimes, or (e) declare that laws made by Parliament should not be obeyed, as King James had done.

The Bill of Rights also included the principles that (a) everyone must obey the law, even the king and Parliament, (b) elections must be free, and (c) the people have the right to keep and carry weapons.

Balanced powers and representative government

You can see how during this relatively short period of time, the balance of power in the English government shifted from the king to the Parliament. The basic idea of representative government had become firmly established. However, only men with property had the right to vote and to be a member of the House of Commons. Most people today would consider the government corrupt because these men often served their own interests at the expense of the common welfare.

In 1707, England and Scotland (which until then had its own parliament) agreed to join together along with Wales to create the kingdom of Great Britain. Therefore, in this book, England is referred to as Great Britain for events occurring after that date.

The British constitutional monarchy

During the colonial period, the British government was becoming increasingly limited in what it could do by a constitution which included the following:

- A set of documents and customs, including the Magna Carta and the English Bill of Rights, which set limits on the powers of the government and spelled out the rights of English freemen.

- A system of responsible government in which ministers appointed by the king were directly responsible to Parliament.

- A system in which the executive, legislative, and judicial powers were separated among the monarchy, Parliament, and the courts.

The "balanced constitution" of the British government was greatly admired in other nations. The French political philosopher Montesquieu called the British government "this beautiful system" because he felt that it was perfectly balanced and, therefore, the only one in the world in which the constitution guaranteed political liberty.

Problem solving

Complete the following chart by identifying an example in British government of each of the basic ideas listed.

Idea	British government
1. Basic rights	
2. Limited government	
3. Separated powers	
4. Shared powers	
5. Consent	
6. Representative government	

To complete this exercise, identify at least one example of how each of the above ideas applies to our present government.

Reviewing and using the lesson

1. What is the Magna Carta? Explain why it is important in the development of constitutional government in England.

2. A struggle between king and Parliament throughout the 17th century was won by the Parliament. Referring to the English Bill of Rights of 1689, list the restrictions placed upon the king's powers that resulted from Parliament's victory.

3. Explain which provisions of the English Bill of Rights are included in our Constitution.

4. Why do you think that the rights that were secured by the movement toward constitutional government were mostly of help to men who owned property? Why weren't women or poor people given these rights?

What basic ideas of constitutional government were found in the colonial governments?

Purpose of Lesson 7

This lesson describes how the basic ideas of constitutional government were used in the American colonies during the 150 years they were under English rule. Studying how these ideas were used in the colonial governments will help you to understand how the Founders came to create the national government we now have.

When you complete this lesson, you should be able to explain how basic ideas of constitutional government were used in the colonial governments. Some new ideas and terms that are contained in this lesson which you should also be able to explain are listed below.

colonial government
common law
magistrate

Loyal subjects of England in America

The . . . law of England is the . . . law of the [colonies] . . . Let an Englishman go where he will, he carries as much of law and liberty with him, as the nature of things will bear. (Opinion of the counsel to the Board of Trade in London, 1720.)

The English colonists who came to the New World considered themselves loyal subjects of England. They brought with them English customs, English laws, and English ideas about good government. For more than 150 years the colonies were ruled by the government of England. However, because they were so far from England, they needed to have their own local governments as well. Since these thirteen colonial governments were ultimately under the control of the English government, their powers were <u>limited</u> and they could not violate the English constitution, laws, traditions, or government policies.

Library of Congress

English colonists settle New England

Basic ideas of constitutional government in the colonial governments

You have learned that by the late 17th century, the government of England included many of the basic ideas about constitutional government that you have studied. England had a constitution, as it does now, that was not a single written document but was made up of the common law, acts of Parliament, and political customs and traditions. The <u>common law</u> of England included unwritten laws based on custom and decisions made by judicial courts that established legal principles over many years. The following basic ideas of English constitutional government were embodied in the governments of the English colonies.

1. Natural Rights.

The laws of the colonial governments were based in part on the idea that the purpose of government was to protect the people's natural rights to life, liberty, and property. This idea was reflected to some extent in the English common law.

It is important, however, in reading the history of this period to realize that legal rights, for example, the right to vote, usually meant the rights of white men who owned a certain amount of property. At the time of the American Revolution, only about 10 percent of the men in Great Britain had the right to vote. People who did not have such rights were (a) women, (b) free white men who did not own property, (c) white men who were indentured servants, (d) free black men, (e) slaves, and (f) Indians. Women, for example, not only did not have the right to vote but, under English law, "the husband and wife are one person. . . the very being or legal existence of the woman is suspended during the marriage."

2. Higher law

This idea is reflected in the general rule that members of the colonial governments could not make any laws or do anything that violated the English constitution. The English law was considered a higher law which was superior to any laws the colonial governments might make.

3. Separation of powers

As in England, to protect the people from the possible abuse of power, the powers of government in the colonies were separated among the following three branches of government.

Library of Congress

The first legislative assembly in America meets in Virginia, 1619

- An <u>executive</u> branch. <u>Governors</u> were responsible for carrying out and enforcing the law. In most of the colonies, by the time of the American revolution, the governors were chosen either by the king or the proprietors. Only in Connecticut and Rhode Island were the governors elected by those men in the colonies who were allowed to vote.

- A <u>legislative</u> branch. All of the colonies had <u>legislatures</u> which were responsible for making laws. Each one was similar to the Parliament in England with an "upper house" like the House of Lords and a "lower house" like the House of Commons. Members of the upper house were either appointed by the governor or elected by the most wealthy property owners of the colony. The lower house was elected by all of the men in the colony who owned a certain amount of property. Pennsylvania was an exception; it only had one house.

- A <u>judicial</u> branch. This branch was made up of judges called <u>magistrates</u> who were usually appointed by the governor. Their responsibility was to handle conflicts over the laws and to preside at trials of those accused of breaking the law. They were also responsible for making sure the colonies were being governed in a way that was consistent with English law and tradition.

4. Checks and balances

Power was separated and in some cases <u>shared</u> among these branches, so that the use of power by one branch of government could be <u>checked</u> by that of another. For example:

- The powers of the <u>governors</u> were <u>checked</u> by (a) their inability to collect taxes without the consent of the legislature, (b) their inability to have persons imprisoned without a trial by a magistrate, and (c) the fact that their salary was often decided upon by the legislature.

- The powers of the <u>legislatures</u> were <u>checked</u> by (a) their having to rely on the governor to enforce the laws that they passed, (b) the power of the magistrates to make sure they did not make laws that violated those of England, and (c) in some colonies, the veto power held by the governor.

- The powers of the <u>magistrates</u> were <u>checked</u> by (a) the fact that they were appointed by the governor, (b) the power of the governor or legislature to remove them if their decisions seemed inappropriate, (c) their reliance on the governor to enforce their decisions, and (d) the basic right of every Englishman to a trial by a jury of his peers from the community.

5. Representative government and the right to vote

Representative government began soon after the first colonies were established. The first representative assembly was held in Virginia as early as 1619. As you have learned, the English Bill of Rights of 1689 gave Englishmen who owned a certain amount of property the right to elect representatives to serve their interests in the House of Commons.

Soon after passing the Bill of Rights, the English Parliament insisted upon applying the idea of representative government in the colonies. At least one house in each colony's legislature was required to be elected by eligible voters.

The right of citizens to elect representatives was seen as a way to (a) reduce the possibility that members of government would violate the people's rights and (b) make sure that at least a part of the government could be counted on to respond to the needs and interests of the people, or at least of those people who had the right to vote.

The colonists' freedom to govern themselves

This lesson has described some of the basic ideas and experiences of English government that the colonists brought with them to North America. They were important because the colonies had a great deal of freedom to govern themselves as they wished. This freedom was a result of their great distance from England. In addition, England was often at war with other European countries and did not have time to supervise the colonies.

As a result, the colonists became used to the idea of having a large voice in their own government. However, after 150 years of being loyal British subjects, a number of events led to the decision to break free of British rule and begin a new nation. Those events are the subject of the next lesson.

Problem solving

Can you identify examples in the colonial governments of the basic ideas you have studied?

Complete the following chart by identifying and explaining where each constitutional idea listed can be found in the governments of the American colonies.

Idea   Where found

1. Basic rights

2. Limited government

3. Separated powers

4. Checks and balances

5. Higher law

Reviewing and using the lesson

1. American colonial leaders considered themselves Englishmen with all the liberties and rights their ancestors had gained. Colonial governments illustrated English ideas of good government. Describe the similarities between the colonial governments and the English government.

2. Since the colonists believed that one of the main purposes of constitutional government was to protect the individual's property rights, they limited the right to vote to those men who owned property. What arguments can you give in support of this policy? What points would you develop if you oppose this policy?

3. For much of American colonial history, the thirteen colonies were allowed a great amount of freedom to govern themselves as they liked. What circumstances in England permitted this?

Why did the colonies want to free themselves from Great Britain?

British cartoon published in 1779 shows America throwing off British control

Library of Congress

Purpose of Lesson 8

As you learned in the last lesson, for more than 150 years the colonies were a part of Great Britain. For much of that time the colonists had few problems with the British government. Eventually, however, the situation became so unsatisfactory that the colonists decided to fight for their independence from the mother country. The reasons for that decision are the subject of this lesson.

As you read the lesson, look for situations in which the colonists claimed the British government violated some of the basic principles of constitutional government. Be prepared to use these ideas to justify a declaration of independence from Great Britain. Additional ideas and terms contained in this lesson that you should be able to explain are listed below.

> ministries
> corrupt government
> Continental Congress
> abuse of power
> Minutemen

Preventing the abuse of power

As you have learned, many people in Europe and the colonies believed that the great strength of the English government was that its powers were separated among different branches that represented different classes of people. They thought that the separation and balance of powers among the different branches would prevent the king, the nobles, or the people themselves from abusing the power of government. However, during the colonial period, a number of events led some people to think the British system of government was not working properly. Some

27

of the most important of these events are described in this lesson.

England becomes a world power

In the late 1600s, England was becoming a powerful nation. It had an army and navy that could exert its power all over the world. It had many colonies that provided it with great wealth and other resources. The larger and more complicated the nation became, the more need there was for an efficient and effective national government.

To improve their ability to govern the nation, Parliament and the king agreed to establish ministries, or departments of government. These were headed by <u>ministers</u>. The ministers' responsibility was to help the king develop new policies and to administer the laws that were passed by Parliament. The king and his ministers made up the <u>executive</u> branch of government.

Charges of corruption in the British government

By the early 1720s there were some people in Great Britain who believed that the executive branch was becoming more powerful than the other branches of government. They were worried that this loss of a proper balance of power among the different branches of government would enable the king and his ministers to gain so much power that they could (a) ignore the limitations placed upon them by the English constitution, (b) violate the rights of the people, and (c) favor their own interests at the expense of the common welfare.

Because of this increase in the power of the executive branch, many critics in Great Britain claimed that the British government was becoming corrupt. It was common for the king to bribe members of Parliament to get them to do what he wanted. He did this by giving them money or by appointing them as ministers or to other positions in the government. The critics pointed to the increases in taxes requested by the ministers and the king and to the large army that the king began to keep. They were concerned that many ministers and the king seemed to be cooperating closely with bankers and businessmen to favor their own selfish interests at the expense of the common welfare. This is exactly what political philosophers meant by corrupt government.

The colonists in America were aware of these criticisms of the British government. However, since that government had left them alone for the most part, they were not, at first, seriously concerned about the warnings of the critics.

The British government tightens control over the colonies

The American colonists did become alarmed when the British government began to develop an increased interest in tightening its control over them. This interest was at least partially because the colonists had been able to get away with not obeying laws made by Parliament which they didn't like, such as the Navigation Acts which controlled their trade.

Also, Great Britain had been at war with France. During this "French and Indian War," the French had used American Indians to help them fight against the British forts and the colonists' settlements in the west.

Protests against the Stamp Act, an early attempt to tax the colonists, 1765

Although Great Britain had won the war, the cost of keeping their troops in America to protect the colonists was high.

Even after the war there was still trouble on the frontier because the colonists were moving westward and taking the Indians' lands. To reduce this problem, the British government ordered the colonists to move back from the frontier. Parliament increased the colonists' taxes to help pay for the costs of keeping British troops in the colonies to protect them from the Indians. And the British government also tightened its control over the colonists' trade.

The colonists begin to resist

Although some colonists accepted these acts of Parliament, a number resisted them. This resistance was, in part, because of new taxes and trade laws, which meant that some colonists were going to lose money. But perhaps a more important reason was that over the years the colonists had become more firmly attached to the idea of representative government.

The colonists were convinced that representative government was the best way to be sure that their government would respect their rights and interests. Since the colonists did not have the right to vote for representatives to serve their interests in the British Parliament, some of them argued that Parliament did not have the right to pass laws taxing them. They thought that tax laws should only be made in their own colonial legislatures where they had the right to vote for representatives to protect their interests. You are probably familiar with the colonists' demand that there be "no taxation without representation."

The fears of some of the leading colonists were increased when the British government continued to tax the colonies and to increase its control over their trade. It passed acts which placed additional import duties and burdens on the colonies. For example, the Quartering Act required the colonists to allow British soldiers to live in their homes. This action increased the colonists' fears of having a large army in the colonies which was controlled by the British government.

Critics in Great Britain had warned about the growing power of the king and his ministers, and of the threat that their control of the army and navy was to the rights of the people. The colonists became more and more alarmed. Their concern over the corruption of the British government was growing stronger, as was their opposition to that government.

The Boston Massacre of 1770 was another event that convinced some of the Americans that the British government was a threat to their rights. A mob of citizens that had attacked a sentry at the Customs House in Boston was fired on by British troops. Seven people were killed. Later, the British soldiers who had been charged with murder were found innocent of the charges. Taxes and duties may have been a subtle sign of tyranny, but killing citizens was

This 1770 engraving by Paul Revere illustrates the Boston Massacre as seen by the colonists

not. The Boston Massacre made the colonists more resistant to British efforts to control them.

The Tea Act of 1773, which actually lowered the tax on tea imported to the colonies, but reasserted the right of Parliament to tax the colonists, was resisted everywhere. The most dramatic resistance was the Boston Tea Party, a raid by colonists masquerading as Indians who boarded British ships in Boston Harbor and threw the tea overboard. The British government responded angrily with what were called by the Americans the Intolerable Acts, which closed Boston harbor to all trade.

Great Britain also weakened representative government in Massachusetts by giving more power to the royal governor, severely limiting town meetings, weakening the court system, and planning for a massive occupation of the colony by British troops.

The colonists organize to resist British control

In the fall of 1774, twelve of the thirteen colonies sent representatives to a meeting in Philadelphia to decide on the best response to the actions of the British government. This meeting was the First Continental Congress. Its members agreed to impose their own ban on trade with Great Britain in an attempt to force the government to change its policies toward the colonies. The British government, however, considered that decision an act of irresponsible defiance of authority and ordered its troops to arrest some leading colonists in Massachusetts.

By this time many of the more radical colonists, especially in New England, were beginning to prepare for war against Great Britain. They believed it was the right of the people to overthrow any government that no longer protected their rights. The colonists formed civilian armies made up of "Minutemen," so called because of their pride in how quickly they could be ready to fight off the British attack that everyone expected.

The revolution begins

On April 19, 1775, British troops tried to march to Concord, Massachusetts, where they had heard that the Minutemen had hidden arms and ammunition. But the colonists learned what was happening. Paul Revere and William Dawes rode through the countryside warning the people that the British were about to attack. On that day, at the towns of Lexington and Concord, war broke out between the colonies and Great Britain--the "shot heard 'round the world" had been fired.

Representatives from the colonies met in Philadelphia in the Second Continental Congress and decided to resist the British. On June 15, 1775, George Washington was chosen to be commander-in-chief of the colonial army. A year later, the Congress asked a committee to draft a document that would explain to the world why the colonists felt that it was necessary to revolt and free themselves from the government that had established the colonies. Thomas Jefferson drafted this document with the assistance of the other members of the committee. It has become known as the Declaration of Independence.

Reviewing and using the lesson

1. Critics of the British government believed it was becoming corrupt. What evidence did they have for their opinion?

2. By the 1760s, American colonists began to resist certain actions of the British government. What were these actions and why did many Americans resist them?

3. The British government, for the most part, believed that its policies in the colonies were fair and just. Develop arguments in support of the British government's point of view.

4. List specific events that led to the American decision to revolt against the British government. For each you select, identify the basic idea about government it violated. Then, develop an argument based upon the ideas and events to justify the American revolution against the British government.

5. Women took an active role in the revolutionary struggle, forming anti-tea leagues and non-importation groups to see that colonists did not buy British goods during the boycott. What does the following quotation tell you about women's views on their role in colonial politics?

> Let the Daughters of Liberty, nobly arise,
> And tho's we've no Voice, but a negative here, The use of the Taxables, let us forbear.

What basic ideas about government are contained in the Declaration Of Independence?

Purpose of Lesson 9

The Declaration of Independence contains many of the basic ideas about government upon which our nation was founded. This lesson will help you understand the argument of the Declaration and how it includes these ideas in its justification of the separation of the colonies from Great Britain.

When you have completed the lesson, you should be able to explain the main arguments contained in the Declaration.

National Portrait Gallery,
Smithsonian Institution

Thomas Jefferson, 1743 - 1826

The colonists list their complaints against the king

Thomas Jefferson was a statesman, a diplomat, an author, an architect, and a scientist. Born in Virginia, Jefferson was a quiet member of the Continental Congress during the early period of the Revolutionary War. He was not known as a great speaker before large groups, but he had a reputation for working well in small committees and was admired for his excellent writing style. Because of his talent for writing, he was chosen to draft the Declaration of Independence.

The Declaration of Independence, adopted by the Continental Congress on July 4, 1776, is the best summary available of the colonists' basic ideas about government and their complaints about British rule that led the Americans to begin the revolution.

In the last lesson, you learned about the colonists' complaints against the British Parliament. However, in the Declaration of Independence, the colonists directed their complaints against the king. This was the first time the colonists had attacked the British king and the idea of monarchies in general.

The main arguments of the Declaration of Independence

The Declaration of Independence was an important turning point in the development of constitutional government in America. The following summarizes some of the main points in its argument.

1. The rights of the people are based on natural law which is a higher law than laws made by men. Neither constitutions nor governments can violate the higher law. If a government violates the law and deprives the people of their rights, they have the right to change or abolish it and form a new government.

2. A compact or agreement existed between the colonists and the king. By the terms of this compact, the colonists consented to be governed by the king so

long as he protected their rights to life, liberty, and property.

3. Since there was no compact between the colonists and Parliament that gave Parliament the right to participate in their governments, Parliament had no right to tax the colonies. This was especially true, argued the colonists, since they did not have the right to send representatives to Parliament.

4. The king had violated the compact by repeatedly acting with Parliament to deprive the colonists of the rights he was supposed to protect. Therefore the colonists had the right to withdraw their consent to be governed by him and to establish their own government.

The Declaration of Independence also sets forth some of the ideals of our constitutional democracy. Much of the history of the United States has been an effort to make these ideals a reality for everyone. In future lessons we will learn how they were gradually gained by blacks, other minorities, and women.

What basic ideas are contained in the Declaration of Independence?

The complete Declaration of Independence, as originally printed, is contained at the end of this text. The following excerpts contain some of its basic ideas. Read them and be prepared to answer the questions that follow.

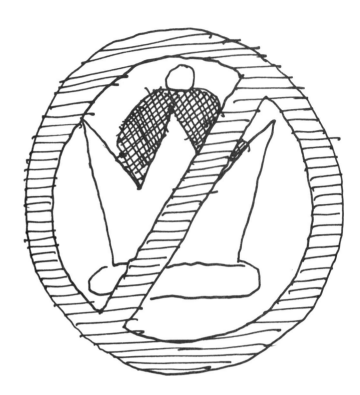

> *We hold these Truths to be self-evident, that all Men are created equal, that they are endowed by their Creator with certain unalienable Rights, that among these are Life, Liberty, and the Pursuit of Happiness--That to secure these Rights, Governments are instituted among Men, deriving their just Powers from the Consent of the Governed, that whenever any Form of Government becomes destructive of these Ends, it is the Right of the People to alter or to abolish it, and to institute new Government, laying its Foundation on such Principles, and organizing its Powers in such Form, as to them shall seem most likely to effect their Safety and Happiness . . . .*

> *The History of the present King of Great-Britain is a History of repeated Injuries and Usurpations, all having in direct Object the Establishment of an absolute Tyranny over these States. To prove this, let Facts be submitted to a candid World . . . .*

> *He has refused to pass other Laws for the Accommodation of large Districts of People, unless those People would relinquish the Right of Representation in the Legislature . . . .*

> *He has dissolved Representative Houses repeatedly, for opposing with manly Firmness his Invasions on the Rights of the People . . . .*

> *He has made Judges dependent on his Will alone . . . .*

> *He has kept among us, in Times of Peace, Standing Armies, without the consent of our Legislatures . . . .*

> *He has combined with others to subject us to a Jurisdiction foreign to our Constitution, and unacknowledged by our Laws; giving his Assent to their Acts of pretended Legislation: For quartering large Bodies of Armed Troops among us: For protecting them, by a mock Trial, from Punishment for any Murders which they should commit on the Inhabitants of these States: For cutting off our Trade with all Parts of the World . . . .*

> *In every stage of these Oppressions we have Petitioned for Redress in the most humble*

Terms: Our repeated Petitions have been answered only by repeated Injury. A Prince, whose Character is thus marked by every act which may define a Tyrant, is unfit to be the Ruler of a free People.

Nor have we been wanting in our Attentions to our British Brethren. We have warned them from Time to Time of Attempts by their Legislature to extend an unwarrantable Jurisdiction over us . . . . They too have been deaf to the Voice of Justice . . . .

We, therefore, the Representatives of the UNITED STATES OF AMERICA, in GENERAL CONGRESS, Assembled, appealing to the Supreme Judge of the world for the Rectitude of our Intentions, do, in the Name, and by the Authority of the good People of these Colonies, solemnly Publish and Declare, That these United Colonies are, and of Right ought to be, FREE AND INDEPENDENT STATES; that they are absolved from all Allegiance to the British Crown, and that all political Connection between them and the State of Great-Britain, is and ought to be totally dissolved . . . .

The committee that drafted the Declaration: Franklin, Jefferson, Adams, Livingston, and Sherman

Examining the Declaration of Independence

1. What is the purpose of government as described in the Declaration of Independence? How is this similar to or different from the purpose of government described by the natural rights philosophers?

2. What does the Declaration say about what people have a right to do if a government is destructive of their rights? How is this related to the ideas of the natural rights philosophers?

3. What do you think Jefferson meant when he said that all men are "endowed by their Creator with certain inalienable Rights"? How is his position related to the natural rights philosophy?

4. What do you think Jefferson meant when he wrote that "all men are created equal?" Did he mean that all had equal ability and character?

5. What basic rights are included in these excerpts from the Declaration of Independence? How are they similar to or different from the rights listed by the natural rights philosophers?

6. The Declaration of Independence is one of most influential writings in history for it contains promises of human rights. Can you think of situations in this century in which it has been used to justify peaceful or violent change?

How were the state constitutions designed to prevent the abuse of power?

Purpose of Lesson 10

Soon after the Revolutionary War started in 1775, the new states began to develop their own written constitutions. Never before had so many new governments been created using the basic ideas of the natural rights philosophy, republicanism, and constitutional government. A review of the main ideas contained in the state constitutions will show you how the Founders designed their state governments to protect their rights and promote the common welfare.

When you complete this lesson, you should be able to explain how the basic ideas about government you have studied were included in the state constitutions. You should also be able to explain the major difference in the way the Massachusetts Constitution was designed to protect rights from the way the constitutions of the other states were designed to protect individual rights. To do so, you will need to be able to explain the following ideas.

> **popular sovereignty**
> **representative government**
> **legislative supremacy**

Six basic ideas included in state constitutions

The experiences of the Founders with the shortcomings of the state governments under their new constitutions greatly influenced the way they wrote the Constitution of the United States. The following describes the basic ideas included in these constitutions and how the Massachusetts constitution differed from those of the other states.

1. Higher law and natural rights

Every state constitution was considered a <u>higher law</u> that must be obeyed by the persons running the government. Each contained the idea that the purpose of government was to preserve and protect citizens' <u>natural rights to life, liberty, and property</u>.

2. Social contract

Each state constitution also made it clear that its government was formed as a result of a <u>social contract</u> --an agreement among its people to create a government to protect their natural rights.

3. Popular sovereignty

All of the state constitutions contained the idea of <u>popular sovereignty</u>--that the people are the source of the authority of the government.

4. Representation and the right to vote

One of the most significant things about each state constitution was the importance placed upon <u>representation</u> of the people in their governments. All of the state constitutions created <u>legislatures</u> that were composed of <u>elected representatives of the people</u>.

In most states, the right to vote for representatives was limited to white males who owned a specified amount of property. However, because it was relatively easy to acquire property in the colonies, this limit on who could vote did not eliminate as many people as it did in Great Britain. In the United States during the period of the American Revolution, about 70 percent of the white males owned enough property to make them eligible to vote. In Great Britain, only about 10 percent were eligible.

In seven states, free blacks and Indians could vote if they met the property requirements. And in New Jersey, the vote was given to "all inhabitants . . . of full age, who were worth fifty pounds" and who met a twelve-month residency requirement. Under these rules, both women and free blacks were able to vote until 1807 when the law in New Jersey was rewritten to exclude women. Twelve states specifically denied women the right to vote by inserting the word "male" into their constitutions.

5. Legislative supremacy

While all of the state constitutions included checks and balances and the separation of powers, most of them relied on a strong legislature and majority rule to protect the rights of the citizens. Legislative supremacy means a government in which most of the power is given to the legislature. Some of the problems raised by legislative supremacy will be discussed in this and other lessons. The reasons for the belief in legislative supremacy were as follows.

- The legislative branch of government, composed of representatives elected by the voters who can also be removed by the voters, is the most democratic branch of government. Therefore, it is considered the safest branch in which to place the most power and the most likely to protect the rights of citizens and to promote their welfare.

- The executive branch should not be trusted with too much power because it is not easily controlled by the people. You may remember that the colonists' greatest problems with the British government had been with its executive branch--the king and his ministers--as well as with the royal governors in the colonies.

- The colonists had also had some difficulty with the judicial branch, the king's magistrates, who tried colonists for breaking British law. However, the power of this branch had been limited by the colonists' right to a trial by a jury

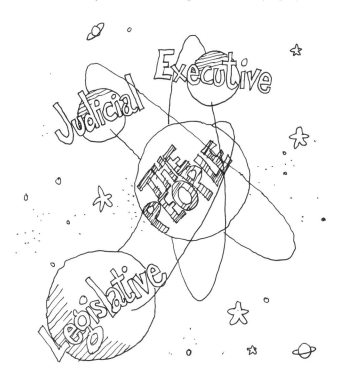

of other colonists. These juries often refused to find them guilty of breaking a law with which the colonists did not agree.

The following evidence of legislative supremacy can be found in the state constitutions.

- The constitutions of most of the states provided for executive branches, but made them dependent on the legislatures. For example, legislatures were given the power to select the governor or to control his salary.

- Governors were allowed to stay in office for only one year. This limit was an attempt to be sure that the governor would not have time to gain much power while in office.

- Appointments made by a governor had to be approved by the legislature.

- Governors were almost totally excluded from the process of lawmaking, which the legislatures kept to themselves. Governors had no power to veto legislation to which they objected.

6. Checks and balances

Although the powers in the state governments were unevenly balanced in favor of strong legislatures, there were some checks in the state constitutions. However, most of these checks existed within the legislatures themselves. For example, in every state except Pennsylvania and Georgia, the legislature was divided into two houses, just as in the British Parliament. Since most important decisions had to be made by both houses, each had a way to check the power of the other house. However, unlike Parliament, and unlike the colonial governments, both houses of the state legislatures were made up of representatives elected by the people. The voters could check their power by electing new representatives to both houses if they did not like the way the government worked.

You may remember that in Parliament, the House of Lords and the House of Commons were designed to represent different classes of people in the British society. This gave each class a way to check the power of the other, if necessary, in order to protect its interests. Some states tried to organize their legislatures in the same way. Only people with a great deal of property could elect representatives to the upper house, while people with less property were allowed to elect representatives to the lower house.

Problem solving

As you have learned, in twelve of the state constitutions the balance of power was heavily weighted in favor of the legislature.

1. How and why was this done?

2. What might be the advantages and disadvantages of this legislative supremacy?

The Massachusetts constitution

In 1780, Massachusetts became the last state to ratify its constitution. Written principally by John Adams, the Massachusetts constitution was different from those of the other states. In addition to relying upon representation as a means of preventing the abuse of power, it also relied upon the traditional methods of separation of powers and checks and balances. It gave the other branches of government more effective checks on the powers of the state legislature than did the other state constitutions. In this way, it contained more similarities to the British government than did the constitutions of the other states.

Perhaps one of the most important reasons the Massachusetts constitution was different was that during the time that it was being developed, problems arose in the states where the legislatures had been given so much power. These problems will be discussed in the next lesson.

John Adams, 1735 - 1826
Library of Congress

Since the Massachusetts constitution is more similar to the present Constitution of the United States than are the other state constitutions, it is worth looking at in some detail. The following outlines some of the most important parts of the Massachusetts constitution.

1. **A strong executive branch**

Under the Massachusetts constitution, the governor was elected by the people. The writers of its constitution believed that because he would be elected by the people, it would be safe to trust him with greater power so that he would be able to protect their rights and welfare.

To enable the governor to be more independent of the legislature and to allow him to check the legislature's use of power, the Massachusetts constitution contained the following provisions.

- The governor's salary was fixed and could not be changed by the legislature.

- The governor had the power to veto laws made by the legislature, and his veto could only be overridden by a two-thirds vote of the legislature.

- The governor could appoint officials to work in the executive branch and judges to the judicial branch with little interference from the legislature.

2. **Representation of different groups in the society**

Several other parts of the Massachusetts constitution show how that government was organized more like the British government than were those of the other states. You may remember that in Great Britain the powers of government were separated among different groups of British society--royalty, nobility, and commons. A basic reason for separating powers among these groups was to prevent one group from completely dominating the others. In the United States there was no royalty or nobility to take their places in a monarchy or a House of Lords. But the Massachusetts constitution divided the people of the state into groups based upon their wealth.

- Only people with a large amount of property could vote to elect the governor.

- People with slightly less property could vote to elect members of the upper house of the state legislature.

- People with the minimum amount of property that enabled them to vote, could vote for members of the lower house.

How was the Massachusetts constitution different from those of the other states?

The Massachusetts constitution provided for a more even balance among the powers of the different branches of government. It did not make the legislature the most powerful branch as it was in the other states. In some ways this difference reveals different beliefs about the best ways to prevent the abuse of power by members of government.

- The constitutions of the other states were based on the idea that <u>representation</u> of the people in a strong state <u>legislature</u> was the best way to protect their rights.

- The Massachusetts constitution was based on the idea that <u>representation</u>, <u>separation of powers</u>, <u>checks</u>, and <u>balances</u> were all essential for the protection of the rights of the people.

Reviewing and using the lesson

1. What ideas stated in the Declaration of Independence were included in the state constitutions written during and after the Revolution?

2. From early colonial days there were property requirements for voting. Do you think these requirements conflict with basic principles of democracy? Explain your answer.

3. Describe the ways by which state constitutions ensured that the legislature would be able to dominate the governor.

4. Why did most state constitutions give most of the powers of government to the legislature at the expense of the executive and judicial branches?

5. The Massachusetts constitution differed in important ways from those of the other states. Describe those differences.

6. What arguments can you make for and against the position taken in the Massachusetts constitution that the best means of protecting citizens from abusive government is by a combination of <u>representation</u>, <u>separation of powers</u>, <u>checks</u>, and <u>balances</u>?

7. Should a governor be chosen by the legislature rather than be elected by the people? Should a governor be allowed to veto measures passed by the legislature? Explain your answers.

8. What arguments can you make for and against the idea of <u>legislative supremacy</u> that was included in most of the state constitutions?

Why did the Founders want to change the Articles of Confederation (1781)?

Purpose of Lesson 11

In 1776, the Second Continental Congress voted to declare the colonies independent of the British government. The thirteen colonies were now independent states. But the states needed to cooperate to fight the war against the powerful British army and navy. So one of the first tasks of the Congress was to organize a national government.

A national government was also necessary to perform all of the activities of government studied in earlier lessons--to control trade among the states, and between the states and foreign nations, and to manage conflicts among the states over such issues as where their borders were to be.

The first government created by the Founders did not work well despite all their knowledge of political philosophy, history, and government. A knowledge of the shortcomings of that government is important in understanding that unless a government is organized properly, it may not work very well. It also helps in understanding why our government is organized as it is.

When you have finished reading and discussing this lesson, you should be able to explain why the newly independent Americans created their first constitution, the Articles of Confederation, as they did. You should also be able to explain the problems of the government under the Articles of Confederation. This lesson also introduces the following new ideas and terms which you should be able to explain.

national government
Articles of Confederation
majority rule
loyalists
factions
Shays' Rebellion

The creation of the Articles of Confederation

In 1776, a committee appointed by the Congress and led by John Dickinson of Pennsylvania wrote a draft of a constitution for the first national government. It was called the Articles of Confederation. But the Americans quickly realized that agreeing on what kind of national government to create would not be easy. Members of the Congress argued on and off for more than a year before they came up with a constitution they could agree to present to the states for approval. Then the states argued about the constitution for four more years before all of them approved it.

Independence National Historical Park

John Dickinson, 1732 - 1808

Two major fears made it difficult for the Founders to agree upon the Articles of Confederation:

- the fear of creating a national government that was too strong

- the fear that some states would have more power than others in the national government

These fears and the solutions developed by the Founders are described below. Review the solutions and be prepared to explain the possible advantages and disadvantages of each.

1. Fear of a strong national government

Once the war against Great Britain had started, each state was like a separate nation with its own constitution and government. To the people, their state was their "country" and all eligible voters could have a voice in government. They could elect members of their communities to represent their interests in their state legislatures. The government was close enough to most citizens so they could even participate in some of its activities.

The Founders agreed they needed a national government. But they were afraid of making one that was too strong. They believed that most of the powers of government should be kept by the states because citizens could control state governments more easily than they could control a national government.

Meanwhile, the states were cooperating in the fight to free themselves from the control of a distant government in Great Britain. The Founders believed that the British government had deprived citizens of their rights, including their right to representation in the affairs of government. Many were afraid that if they agreed to create a strong national government, it could dominate the state governments and might become as dangerous to the rights of citizens as the British government had proved to be.

The solution: create a weak national government

The Founders finally arrived at a solution to this problem: they created a weak national government. The government created by the Articles of Confederation was just a national legislature, the Continental Congress. There was no executive or judicial branch. While Congress was permitted to establish courts for certain limited purposes, most legal disputes were handled in state courts.

The Articles of Confederation left most of the powers of government with the states; the national government had little power over the states and their citizens. For example:

- The Continental Congress did not have the power to control any person in any state. Only the state governments had power over their citizens.

- The Continental Congress did not have the power to collect taxes from the states or from the people directly. It could only request money from the state governments, which were supposed to raise the money from their citizens.

- No important decision could be made by the Continental Congress unless at least nine of thirteen states approved. This limitation on the powers of Congress applied, for example, to its ability to declare and conduct war, enter into treaties or alliances with other nations, and coin or borrow money.

2. Fear that some states would dominate others in the national government

The leaders in each state wanted to make sure that the new national government would be organized in a way that would not threaten their state's interests. As a result, the most important disagreement was over how states would vote in Congress. Would each state have an equal vote, or would states with greater population or wealth be given more votes than others? Decisions in the Congress would be made by majority vote. Some leaders were afraid that the majority would use their power for their own interest at the expense of those who were in the minority.

The solution: give each state one vote

The solution adopted was to give each state one vote in the Continental Congress regardless of its population.

In 1781, after four years of discussion, all of the state governments agreed to accept the Articles of Confederation as the constitution for the national government of the United States. For the first time since the term was used in the Declaration of Independence, the former colonies became officially known as the "United States of America."

Problems caused by the weaknesses of the Articles of Confederation

You have seen how the people of the states solved the problem of their fear of a strong national government: they created a government that had very limited power. Because the states were afraid that the Continental Congress might be able to control them, they made sure that they controlled it. Every action taken by the Continental Congress had to be with the consent, approval, and cooperation of most of the states. As a result, the nation began with a very weak national government.

The difficulties that arose under the Articles of Confederation led to the decision to develop our present Constitution. They are described below.

1. No money and no power to get it

Congress had to rely upon voluntary contributions from the state governments to pay for the costs of the national government. It had no power to force the states to live up to their promises to make the contributions.

This system did not work. The states had promised to give the national government $10 million to pay for the costs of fighting the Revolutionary War. They only paid $1.5 million. Congress had borrowed most of the money it needed to pay for the war by selling revenue bonds to Americans and foreigners, and it had no way to pay its debts. The state governments and many of the people living in the states were also deeply in debt after the war.

2. No power over the state governments and their citizens

Congress did not have the power to make laws regulating the behavior of citizens or the states or to force state governments or their citizens to do anything. The citizens could be governed only by their own state governments. This meant that if members of a state government or citizens within a state disobeyed a resolution, recommendation, or request made by the national government, there was no way the national government could make them obey. The Articles clearly stated that each state kept its "sovereignty, freedom, and independence."

The national government's inability to make state governments and their citizens live up to treaties it had made led to a serious situation. Not all of the colonists had been in favor of the Revolutionary War; some had remained loyal to Great Britain. Thousands of these people, called loyalists, still lived in the United States. When the war was over, the national government signed a peace treaty with Great Britain called the Treaty of Paris, which was intended in part to protect loyalists' rights and ensure that they were treated fairly. Some of these loyalists owned property in the states and some had loaned money to other citizens.

Some state governments refused to respect this treaty. They often made it difficult for loyalists to collect the money owed to them by other citizens. Sometimes the states had confiscated the loyalists' property during the war. The national government had no power to force the state governments to respect the property rights of the loyalists or to force individual citizens to pay back money owed to the loyalists. Thus, the national government was powerless to live up to its promise to the British government to protect the rights of these citizens.

3. Unenforceable trade agreements

Although Congress had the power to make agreements with foreign nations, it did not have the power to make state governments live up to these agreements. This raised another difficulty. Some citizens imported goods from other nations and then refused to pay for them. Not surprisingly, people in foreign countries became reluctant to trade with people in the United States. In addition, when Great Britain recognized how weak Congress was in controlling foreign trade, it closed the West Indies to American commerce. As a result, many Americans lost money because they were unable to sell their goods to people in other nations. Others were not able to buy goods from abroad.

4. Unfair competition among the states

Congress had no power to make laws controlling business or trade among the states. As a result, people in some states, often with the help of their state governments, tried to take advantage of people in other states. For example, in order to benefit local businesses, some state governments passed laws forbidding the sale of goods from other states.

Such activities prevented efficient and productive trade among the states and caused serious economic problems for the country. Businesses failed, and many people became poverty-stricken and unable to repay money they had borrowed from other citizens. This created another serious situation.

5. Threats to citizens' right to property

Many people believed that one of the most serious problems in the United States during the 1780s was the failure of the state governments to protect their citizens' property rights. As you have learned, in most states the government was controlled by the legislative branch, composed of representatives elected by a majority of the people.

A <u>faction</u> is a group of people that seeks to promote its own interests. During this period, a number of factions developed that sometimes formed majorities in the state legislatures. These majorities were accused of making laws that benefited themselves at the expense of the minority and of the common welfare. For example, they passed laws that canceled debts, confiscated the property of loyalists, and created paper money resulting in inflation which benefited the debtors at the expense of those to whom they owned money.

People who were being hurt by such laws argued that their property was not being protected by their state governments. They claimed that the state governments were being used by one class of people to deny the rights of others and that they were not acting for the common good.

Some people argued that there was too much democracy in the state governments. They claimed that representative government with majority rule did not adequately protect the natural rights of individual citizens or the common welfare. They argued that <u>majority rule</u>, when the majority pursued its own selfish interests at the expense of the rights of others, was just another form of tyranny, every bit as dangerous as that of an uncontrolled king.

Shays' Rebellion and the seeds of change

A dramatic event that finally convinced many people of the need for a stronger national government was <u>Shays' Rebellion</u>. Farmers in Massachusetts had serious economic problems. When they could not pay their debts, many of them lost their homes and their farms. Some were even put into prison. Popular discontent rose, and angry crowds prevented the courts from punishing people or selling the property of those who could not pay their debts.

In November, 1786, a group of several hundred angry farmers gathered under the leadership of Daniel Shays. Because they needed weapons to use in their rebellion against the state government, they tried to capture the arsenal at Springfield, where arms were kept for the state militia. Although Shays' men were defeated, their rebellion frightened many property owners who feared similar problems might arise in their states.

The fears raised by such conflicts as Shays' Rebellion, combined with the difficulties in raising taxes and regulating foreign trade, convinced a growing number of people of the need to strengthen the national government. George Washington was one of these people. He wrote to James Madison, "We are either a united people or we are not. If the former, let us act as a nation. If we are not, let us no longer act a farce by pretending to it."

The steps taken to create a stronger national government and the way in which it was organized are the subject of the next unit.

Angry farmers, led by Daniel Shays, seize a court house, 1786

Reviewing and using the lesson

1. The Articles of Confederation showed its writers' fears of a strong national government and left most important powers to the states. What important powers were denied the national government by the Articles?

2. Why do you suppose the smaller states were satisfied with the government set up by the Articles of Confederation?

3. How might the experience of the Founders with the state governments have affected their belief in the importance and role of <u>civic virtue</u> in a republic?

4. Select several national problems in the period after the Revolution and show how the lack of power of the national government under the Articles of Confederation contributed to them.

5. The Articles of Confederation demonstrated a distrust of a strong national government. Many people today share this attitude toward national power. Do you believe it is justified? Why?

6. What are "factions"? Explain why they were considered a problem for American government in the 1780s. What organized groups that exist today would the Founders call factions?

Unit Three: The Constitution

Howard Chandler Christy

The signing of the Constitution, at Philadelphia, September 17, 1787

Purpose of Unit Three

You have studied the philosophical and historical influences on the Framers of our Constitution. This unit will provide you with an understanding of how they wrote the Constitution and some of the most important debates they had over its development and ratification.

When you have completed this unit, you should be able to explain how the Constitution was developed, how it organizes our government, some of the basic debates that occurred during its development, and the positions of the Federalists and Anti-Federalists in the struggle over the ratification of the Constitution.

Who attended the Philadelphia Convention and what had they agreed to do?

Independence Hall, Philadelphia site of the convention

Purpose of Lesson 12

The Constitution was written at a convention held in Philadelphia in 1787. This lesson describes how the convention came to be held, some of the most important people who attended it, and some of the first steps they took to create our present Constitution.

When you complete this lesson, you should be able to describe the steps leading to the calling of the Philadelphia Convention and the characteristics of the Framers who attended it. Some of the basic terms it contains which you should be able to explain are listed below.

Philadelphia Convention
delegate
ratification
The Federalist

Attempts to solve the problems of the Articles of Confederation

As a result of the problems experienced under the Articles of Confederation, a number of prominent leaders suggested holding a meeting of representatives of all of the states. The purpose of the meeting was to discuss ways in which these problems could be solved. James Madison of Virginia persuaded his state legislature to call for such a meeting.

In 1786, all thirteen states were invited to send representatives to a meeting in Annapolis, Maryland. Only five states sent representatives. Disappointed at the turnout at the meeting, Madison and the others decided not to discuss the Articles of Confederation. Instead, they wrote a report which they sent to Congress and every state legislature. The report asked each state to send representatives to a meeting that was to be held in Philadelphia in 1787. The purpose of the Philadelphia meeting was to change the Articles of Confederation in order to strengthen the national government.

Congress approves a meeting to improve the Articles of Confederation

At first, Congress ignored the report. Then, in February of 1787, Congress voted to support the meeting of the state representatives. However, it only gave them the authority to develop a plan to improve the Articles of Confederation. This plan was then to be sent to Congress for it to use as it wished. As far as Congress was concerned, the men who met in Philadelphia were just advisers to Congress.

Who attended the Philadelphia Convention?

Fifty-five delegates attended the meeting which later became known as the Philadelphia Convention. It was a remarkable group of men that we now call the Framers of the Constitution. Most of them were fairly young. The average age was forty-two. The youngest delegate was only twenty-seven. About three-fourths of the Framers had served in Congress. Most had been prominent in their states, where many had held political positions. Most had played important parts in the Revolution. Some were rich, but most were not. A French diplomat in America at the time said that the Framers "without being rich are all in easy circumstances."

Another French diplomat stationed in America observed: "If all of the delegates named for the Philadelphia convention are present, one will never have seen, even in Europe, an assembly more respectable for talents, knowledge, disinterestedness, and patriotism than those who will compose it." From Paris, Thomas Jefferson wrote to John Adams in London that the convention "really is an assembly of demigods."

We should remember, however, that some of the Framers were men of modest abilities and questionable motives. Probably the most balanced view of the men at Philadelphia has been given by Max Farrand, a historian, who wrote: "Great men there were, it is true, but the convention as a whole was composed of men such as would be appointed to a similar gathering at the present time: professional men, business men, and gentlemen of leisure; patriotic statesmen and clever, scheming politicians; some trained by experience and study for the task before them; and others utterly unfit. It was essentially a representative body."

Most of the stories of the Framers are worth telling in detail. But we will limit ourselves to introducing you to some of the most important. We will also mention some of the leaders who did not attend but who played a part in the establishment of our constitutional government.

George Washington

George Washington was probably the most respected and honored man in the country. During the Revolutionary War he had left his farm at Mount Vernon, Virginia, to lead the American army to victory over the British. When the war was over and there was no longer a need for a large army, Washington returned to private life on his plantation. He was one of the leading citizens who were convinced that a stronger national government was necessary. But he expressed this opinion only in private and only to a few people, because he was not interested in getting involved in politics.

At first, Washington refused to accept the invitation to attend the convention. Later, he agreed to be a representative from Virginia. He agreed because he feared that if he did not attend, people might think that he had lost his faith in republican government. Washington was not active in the debates, but his presence and his support of the Constitution were essential to its ratification by the states. When the time came to select their first president, there was no one else that Americans could unite behind other than this honorable man who, time and time again, had set aside his own interests and devoted himself to the common welfare of the nation.

George Washington, 1732 - 1799

James Madison

James Madison, of all the Framers, probably had the greatest influence on the organization of the national government that was developed at the convention. Born in 1751, Madison was one of the youngest of the revolutionary leaders. He became active in Virginia politics in the 1780s and was one of the most influential leaders in favor of a stronger national government. His influence at the convention was great in part because he brought with him a plan that he had already developed for creating a better national government--the Virginia Plan. After some debate over alter-

44

natives, this plan was used as the basis for discussion about how to improve the government.

Had it not been for Madison, we probably would not know much about what happened during the convention. The Framers had decided to keep the discussions of the meetings secret, but they trusted Madison to take notes during the proceedings. Most of what we know today about what happened is based on those notes.

After the convention, Madison's convincing arguments about the best way to organize the new government led him to be one of three men asked to write a defense of the newly written Constitution. This defense was a series of articles written for newspapers in New York. It is now called *The Federalist*. It was used to convince the citizens of New York to vote for delegates to the state ratifying convention who were favorable to the Constitution. It is the most important work written by Americans on the basic principles and ideas underlying our constitutional government. Madison later became the fourth President of the United States.

Other important delegates

In addition to Washington and Madison, the delegates included many other prominent men. Benjamin Franklin was 81 and in poor health, but because he was so well respected, his participation at crucial moments contributed a great deal to the success of the Convention. Alexander Hamilton, while one of the greatest supporters of a strong national government, left in frustration before the Convention was half over, returning for a few days and to sign the completed document in September. However, as you will learn in a later lesson, he was one of the authors of *The Federalist* and played a major role in the struggle over the ratification of the Constitution. George Mason, the author of the Virginia Bill of Rights, was a great champion of the rights of the people and of the states. He believed the national government created by the Constitution threatened those rights. He was one of the three delegates who refused to sign the Constitution at the close of the convention.

Important Founders who did not attend the convention

There were also some important political leaders who did not attend the convention.

Thomas Jefferson had drafted the Declaration of Independence, served as governor of Virginia, and was a member of Congress under the Articles of Confederation. At the time of the convention he was ambassador to France and was unable to attend.

Thomas Paine, 1737 - 1809

Thomas Paine, the author of *Common Sense* and *The Rights of Man*, was with Jefferson in France.

John Adams, one of America's most important political thinkers and the second President of the United States, was on a diplomatic mission to England.

Patrick Henry, revolutionary leader, refused to attend the convention because he was against the development of a strong national government. He suspected what might happen at the convention, and said that he "smelled a rat." Henry was one of the leaders who campaigned against adoption of the Constitution.

The convention begins

By May 25, 1787, delegates from a majority of the states were present in Philadelphia. George Washington was unanimously elected to be the presiding officer.

Almost immediately the Framers agreed on two things:

1. They decided to ignore the instructions they had received from Congress to limit their work to improving the Articles of Confederation. Instead, they began to work on the development of a new constitution. The Framers were convinced that the defects of the Articles were so serious that it would be better not to use them as the basis for their discussion.

2. They decided to keep the record of what they said at the convention a secret for thirty years. There were two reasons for this.

- The Framers wanted to develop the best constitution they could. This required a free exchange of ideas. They were afraid that if their debates were made public, many of the delegates would not feel free to express their opinions.

- The Framers thought that the constitution they developed would have a greater chance of being accepted if people did not know about the arguments that went on while it was being created.

The Framers also agreed that although the delegations from each state varied in size, each state would have one vote at the convention.

The Framers were committed to the development of a strong national government. During the convention there was a great deal of agreement on fundamental principles and most of the basic issues. As a result, the Framers were able, in less than four months, to create a constitution that has lasted for two hundred years. This remarkable achievement began with a first session at which only seven of the thirteen states had delegates present. By the end of the convention every state except Rhode Island was represented.

The next lessons will help you understand the Constitution they developed and the basic reasons for its main features.

Reviewing and using the lesson

1. What was the original purpose for calling a meeting in Philadelphia in 1787? Why was the purpose changed?

2. Describe the members of the Philadelphia Convention as a group.

3. Were the members of the Philadelphia Convention right to ignore their original instructions? Why?

4. Why did the Framers decide to keep the debates in the convention a secret for so long?

5. Should the debates at the Philadelphia Convention have been open to the public? Why?

Why did the Framers use the Virginia Plan to create the new Constitution?

Purpose of Lesson 13

Both the Virginia and New Jersey delegates to the Philadelphia Convention submitted plans for the Framers' consideration. After considerable debate, the Virginia Plan was used as the basis for the new Constitution. However, not all of the recommendations of the plan were accepted. An understanding of both plans and the debates over them should increase your understanding of the Constitution and the continuing debates over how our government is organized.

When you finish this lesson, you should be able to explain the differences between the Virginia and New Jersey plans. You should also be able to explain why the Virginia Plan was used as the basis for our Constitution. Several new ideas and terms are introduced in this lesson which you should be able to explain. They are:

federal system
proportional representation
equal representation

The need to create a new constitution

The Framers who met in Philadelphia faced the problem of deciding upon the best way to organize the national government. They wanted to give it enough power to deal effectively with the nation's needs and to protect their rights and promote their welfare. But they also wanted to make sure it would not be able to abuse its powers. Many of the Framers had decided before coming to the convention that they did not want to be limited to improving the Articles of Confederation. They were convinced of the need to create a new constitution.

The Virginia Plan

James Madison was one of those who thought they should develop a new constitution. Before the convention, he had already drafted a plan for a new national government, called the Virginia Plan. He was able to get the delegates to accept this plan as the basis for their discussions about the new government and the writing of a new constitution.

The most important thing to know about the Virginia Plan is that it created a national government. Under the Articles of Confederation, the central government could only act upon the states, not upon the people directly. It could request money, for example, but only the states had the authority to raise that money by placing taxes upon the citizens. Under Madison's plan, the national government would have the power to collect its own taxes, to make laws, and to enforce them in its own courts. Each citizen would then be under two governments, the national government and a state government. And, both of these governments would get their authority from the people. The existence of two governments, national and state, each given a certain amount of authority, is what we now call a <u>federal system</u>. It was a new way to organize a government. In addition, the Virginia Plan provided that:

- The national government would be composed of three branches: legislative, executive, and judicial. The legislative branch would be more powerful than the other branches because, among other things, it would be responsible for selecting people to serve in the executive and judicial branches.

- The legislative branch was to include a Congress with two houses. A <u>House of Representatives</u> would be elected directly by the people of each state. A <u>Senate</u> would be elected by the members of the House of Representatives from lists of persons nominated by the legislatures of each state government.

- The number of representatives from each state in both the House and the Senate would be based on the size of its population. This system of <u>proportional representation</u> meant that states with larger populations would have more representatives in each house of Congress than states with smaller populations. If a state had twice as many people as another state, it would have twice as many votes in Congress. Under this system, the government represented and acted directly upon the people, not the states, as the central government had done under the Articles of Confederation in which each state delegation to Congress had only one vote.

The Virginia Plan gave the legislative branch of the national government the power:

- to make all laws that individual states were unable to pass, such as laws which regulated trade between two or more states.

- to strike down laws of the state legislatures that it considered to be in violation of the national constitution or the national interest.

- to call forth the armed forces of the nation against a state, if necessary, to enforce the laws passed by Congress.

- to elect people to serve in the executive and judicial branches of government.

Reactions to the Virginia Plan

There was considerable debate among the Framers over the Virginia Plan. Most agreed that representation in the House of Representatives should be based on population. The main disagreement was about how many representatives each state could send to the Senate. The different positions were as follows.

- The <u>larger states</u> wanted the Senate also to be based on proportional representation. This would mean they would be able to send more representatives to the Senate than the smaller states. They would then have more power than the smaller states in both the Senate and the House of Representatives.

- The <u>smaller states</u> wanted the Senate to be organized so that each state, no matter how many people lived in it, would have <u>equal representation.</u> Thus, at least in the Senate, no state would have more power than any other state. The position of the small states was based on their fear that unless they had an equal voice in the Senate, the larger states would use the powers of the national government against them.

This debate created a major problem. The Framers from New Jersey, a small state, asked for time to come up with their own plan to be used as the basis for discussion on how to organize the new government.

The New Jersey Plan

The Framers from New Jersey and the other states with smaller populations were afraid that the Virginia Plan would create a national government in which they had little power. They argued that the safest and fairest thing to do would be to improve the Articles of Confederation. The New Jersey plan was a way to do this. The following are some of the main parts of the plan.

1. **Legislative branch.**

Congress would have only one house with each state having equal representation; and it would be given increased powers such as the following.

- <u>Taxes</u>. The national government would be given the power to levy certain taxes such as import duties to raise money for its operations, along with the power to collect money from states if they refused to pay.

- Trade. Congress would be given the power to control trade among the states and with foreign nations.

- Control over the states. The laws and treaties with foreign nations made by Congress would be considered to be the supreme law of the nation. No state could make laws that were contrary to these laws.

2. Executive branch

This branch would be made up of several persons selected by Congress. They would have the power to administer national laws, appoint other executive officeholders, and direct all military operations.

3. Judicial branch

A supreme court would be appointed by the leaders of the executive branch. It would have power to handle conflicts over treaties, trade among the states or with foreign nations, and the collection of taxes.

Problem solving

Which was the better plan?

The Virginia and New Jersey plans each had certain benefits and costs. Understanding these is helpful in making intelligent decisions about which is the better plan. Complete the chart below to illustrate the benefits and costs of the two plans. Then select the plan which, in your analysis, would be the better plan for establishing the legislative branch of the government. Explain the reasons for your decision.

Virginia Plan		New Jersey Plan	
Benefits	Costs	Benefits	Costs

Why was the Virginia Plan used?

Basically, the New Jersey Plan continued the system of government existing under the Articles of Confederation. In this system, the central government represented and acted upon the states rather than directly representing and acting upon the people. The New Jersey Plan did contain useful suggestions to solve some of the weaknesses of the Articles of Confederation. If these suggestions had been made at the begin-

ning of the meeting in Philadelphia, they might have been accepted by everyone except those who were the most committed to having a very strong national government. If that had happened, the new constitution might not have been developed.

But by the time the New Jersey Plan was presented, two weeks after the Virginia Plan, many of the delegates had become convinced that they should create a strong national government. Madison's Virginia Plan became the basis for that government. As it was, the New Jersey Plan was supported only by the delegates from that state, by those from New York and Delaware, and by part of the Maryland delegation.

However, two major issues had not been resolved:

- How should the number of representatives from each state be determined? According to its population? Many delegates still argued that each state should have an equal number of votes, no matter how large or small its population was.

- What powers should the national government have?

There were serious disagreements on these issues among the Framers from states with large populations, states with small populations, and states with slaves. These disagreements were so intense that the convention almost failed at this time. How these issues were resolved is the subject of the next lesson.

Reviewing and using the lesson

1. List five major points of Madison's Virginia Plan. For each point that you select, state how it differed from the existing arrangement under the Articles of Confederation.

2. The most important difference of opinion at the convention was between delegates from the large and small states. On what issue did they differ? Why?

3. What do you see as the crucial difference between the New Jersey Plan and the Virginia Plan? Why was the Virginia Plan, with changes, chosen by the delegates as the basis for the new government?

4. Why do you suppose the Virginia Plan gave Congress the right to strike down laws made by state legislatures? What arguments could you make for or against giving Congress this power?

How did the Framers develop the legislative branch and what powers did they give it?

The Old Senate Chamber as it appeared in 1859

Purpose of Lesson 14

This lesson explains how and why Congress is organized into two houses, why each state can select two senators, and why representation in the House of Representatives is based on population. The lesson also explains some of the powers of Congress. It concludes with a discussion of some of the disagreements that separated the delegates of the northern and southern states.

When you complete this lesson, you should be able to explain how and why the present basis of representation in Congress came to be and the advantages and disadvantages of the system. You should also be able to explain the following ideas and terms contained in this lesson.

> equal representation
> proportional representation
> The Great Compromise (Connecticut Compromise)
> enumerated powers
> necessary and proper clause
> supremacy clause
> guarantee clause
> ex post facto laws
> three-fifths clause
> fugitive slave clause

How should Congress be organized?

Once the Virginia Plan was accepted, there was still the problem of deciding how to organize the new government in a way that would be acceptable to most of the Framers. The first debates were about what responsibilities and powers should be given to Congress and how it should be organized. The result of the Framers' efforts was the development of Article I of our Constitution. The basic problems the Framers had in developing Article I are set forth below. Some of the problems the Framers discussed are still being debated today.

The problem of representation

After the defeat of the New Jersey Plan, the Framers from the states with smaller populations became increasingly afraid that the new national government would be dominated by the larger states. Their solution was to insist that each state have the same number of representatives in the Congress--the position called <u>equal representation</u>. They were also convinced that the people in their states would never approve the Constitution if it did not preserve the idea that all states should be treated equally.

The delegates from the states with larger populations thought this was not fair. They argued that a state with a larger number of people should have a greater voice (that is, more votes) in the decisions of the national government--the position called <u>proportional representation.</u>

The Framers were asked to vote whether there should be equal or proportional representation in the Senate. Half of the Framers voted one way and the other half voted the other. They could not reach a decision. Neither side was willing to compromise. Just a few weeks after the convention had begun, the Framers were in serious disagreement and almost ready to quit and go home.

At this time a special committee was formed of one delegate from each state. This committee was responsible for trying to develop a plan to save the situation. Some of the strongest supporters of the Virginia Plan, such as James Madison and James Wilson, a delegate from Pennsylvania, were against giving this responsibility to a committee. However, most of the Framers disagreed with them and the committee went to work.

Problem solving

How many representatives should each state send to Congress?

Your class should be divided into committees of about five students each. Each committee should contain some students who represent the small states and some who represent the large states. The task of each committee is as follows.

1. Meet and develop a plan for how many representatives each state should be allowed to send to the Senate and to the House of Representatives.

2. Select a spokesperson to present its plan to the entire class. Then, all members of the committee may help to clarify its plan and defend it against criticisms by members of other committees.

3. Each committee may then revise its plan if it wishes, and put it on the chalkboard or chart paper.

The entire class should then compare the plans made by the committees and try to reach an agreement on a plan. After you have completed this exercise, compare the plans you have developed with the plan arrived at by the Framers, which is described below.

The Great Compromise

The result of the committee's work at the Philadelphia Convention is known both as the Great Compromise and the Connecticut Compromise. Its solution, first suggested by Benjamin Franklin, contained the following proposals:

- The House of Representatives would be elected on the basis of proportional representation.

- There would be equal representation of each state in the Senate. The legislature of each state would select the two senators from that state.

- The House of Representatives would be given the power to develop all bills for taxing and government spending. The Senate was limited

to either accepting or rejecting these bills but, as originally proposed, it could not change them. This was later changed to permit the Senate to amend "money bills" developed in the House.

As in most compromises, each side received a little and gave up a little. The small states received the equal representation in the Senate that their delegates wanted in order to protect their interests. The large states gave up control of the Senate but kept their control of the House of Representatives. And the House was given important powers regarding taxation and government spending.

The result was that the large states would have slightly more influence over the creation of laws regarding taxation and how the money would be spent by the government. However, the decisions of the House of Representatives would always be subject to the check of the Senate, in which the small states had equal representation.

When the committee presented this compromise to the other Framers, it was bitterly fought by some members from the larger states, including Madison, Wilson, and Gouverneur Morris, an important delegate from Pennsylvania. The debate became so heated that two of the New York delegates left the convention and did not return. However, the crisis passed when the compromise was passed by the delegates--by one vote.

The powers of Congress - Article I of the Constitution

The Framers intended the new government to be a government of enumerated, or specifically listed, powers. They thought it was important to list the powers of Congress so that there would not be any confusion about what Congress could and could not do. The list of what Congress can do appears in Article I, Section 8 of the Constitution. It includes such important matters as the power to lay and collect taxes in order to "pay the debts and provide for the common defence and general welfare of the United States . . . ," to declare war, and to raise an army and navy.

The necessary and proper clause

In addition to the powers the Framers specifically listed for the Congress, they added at the end of the list the power to make all other laws that are "necessary and proper" for carrying out the enumerated powers. This is called the necessary and proper clause. It is an important part of the Constitution that you will learn about later.

Controlling the state governments

One of the main reasons the Framers agreed to meet in Philadelphia was their concern over actions some of the state governments were taking. They wanted to create a national government that would be able to limit the powers of the state governments, in part because these state governments did not always obey the central government's decisions under the Articles of Confederation. And the central government did not have the power to enforce its decisions.

All of the Framers agreed that they had to create a national government that had more power than it had under the Articles of Confederation. However, they did not agree about how much power it should have over the state governments and their citizens.

The power of the national government over state governments and the people

The primary solution that was finally adopted was the creation of a national government with the authority to act directly on the people. This meant that the national government was no longer dependent on the states for the collection of the taxes it levied or the enforcement of the laws it passed. The Framers also included a number of phrases or clauses in the Constitution that set forth the powers of the national government over state governments and the people. Some of the most important of these are listed below.

1. The supremacy clause states that the Constitution and all laws made by Congress are the supreme law of the land. The executive branch is given the power to enforce these laws. The Supreme Court is given the power to handle conflicts over their application and interpretation.

2. Article IV of the Constitution gives the national government the authority to guarantee each state a republican form of government.

3. Article IV also requires the national government to protect the states from invasion or domestic violence. This important grant of power is known as the guarantee clause.

Limits on the powers of state government

The Constitution includes several limitations on the powers of state government. Some of the most important of these are listed below.

1. Article I prohibits state governments from:

- creating their own money

- passing laws that enable people to violate contracts such as those between creditors and debtors

- making ex post facto laws, laws which make acts crimes even though the acts were legal at the time they were committed

- entering into treaties with foreign nations or declaring war

- granting titles of nobility

2. Article IV prohibits states from:

- unfairly discriminating against citizens of other states

- refusing to return fugitives from justice to the states from which they have fled

Problems that separated the northern and southern states

The Great Compromise had settled the disagreement between the large and small states over how many representatives they could send to the Senate and the House of Representatives. But another issue had to be resolved. This was the conflict between the interests of the states dependent on slave labor and those where slavery was forbidden.

Slavery had been practiced for almost as long as there had been colonies in America. Most of the Framers were opposed to slavery. Still, people in the south used slaves as workers. Slaves were considered personal property, and slaveowners wanted to continue to be able to use them. Delegates from some of these states informed the others that their states would refuse to be a part of the new national government if it denied citizens the right to import slaves. If the Constitution interfered with the slave trade, North Carolina, South Carolina, and Georgia made it clear that they would not become a part of the new nation.

Compromises made to get southern states to sign the Constitution

After considerable debate, the Framers agreed on a way to satisfy both the northern non-slaveowning interests and the southern slaveowners. This agreement gave Congress the power to regulate interstate commerce which the northern states wanted. In order to satisfy the demands of the southern states, a guarantee was written into the Constitution that the national government would not interfere with the slave trade until at least 1808.

The "three-fifths clause"

In addition, each slave was to be counted as three-fifths of a person in determining how many representatives a state could send to the House of Representatives. Article I of the Constitution provided that direct taxes must be in proportion to the population. Again, each slave was to be counted as three-fifths of a person for purposes of taxation. This is the famous "three-fifths clause."

The "fugitive slave clause"

Finally, the "fugitive slave clause" of Article IV provided that slaves who escaped to other states must be returned to their owners. These provisions of the Constitution, designed to satisfy the demands of the slave-owning states, were not matters of great controversy. In 1787, although there was much opposition to slavery, it was not yet the major issue it was later to become.

New York Public Library

Slave auctions, such as this one in Virginia, disturbed many northerners and was an issue for compromise at the Convention

Reviewing and using the lesson

1. The major difference of opinion at the Constitutional Convention was over the question of representation in the legislative branch of the new government. What was this difference? How was it resolved?

2. Certain powers are denied to the states by the Constitution. Name several.

3. According to the Constitution, what is the supreme law of the land? Whose responsibility is it to enforce the laws of the United States?

4. Why did the Framers decide to make a list of the powers that Congress would be allowed to exercise? What clause did they attach to the end of that list that was not specific? Why did they do so?

5. What disagreements do you think might arise over the interpretation of the clause that said that Congress was given the power to make all laws which were necessary and proper for fulfilling its responsibilities as outlined in the Constitution? Why?

6. What compromises of differences between northern and southern states were written into the Constitution? Would you have supported these compromises even though they accepted the institution of slavery? Why?

7. Are there good arguments today in support of the constitutional requirement that all states be equally represented in the Senate? If so, what are they?

8. Are there good arguments today in support of dividing Congress into two bodies--a Senate and House of Representatives? If so, what are they?

How did the Framers develop the executive and judicial branches and what powers did they give these branches?

Washington, the most admired man in America, was the logical choice for president

Purpose of Lesson 15

This lesson explains how the Framers organized the executive and judicial branches of the government. It also describes the difficulties the delegates had in deciding how best to control the power of the executive, and how and why they created an unusual method of selecting the president. Finally, it describes the responsibilities given to the judicial branch.

When you finish this lesson, you should be able to explain how the Constitution organizes the executive and judicial branches. This should include an explanation of the limits on the powers of the executive. New ideas and terms included in this lesson which you should be able to explain are listed below.

> **impeach**
> **electoral college**
> **electors**
> **original jurisdiction**
> **appellate jurisdiction**

Limiting the power of the executive

The Framers wanted to give the executive branch enough power to fulfill its responsibilities. However, they did not want to give the executive branch so much power that it could easily be abused. Americans, and many Englishmen, believed that the king, through the use of bribes and special favors, had been able to control elections and exercise too much influence over the Parliament. They thought his actions upset the proper balance of power between the king and Parliament. It was the destruction of this balance that Americans referred to when they spoke of the corruption of the Parliament by the king. In addition, they believed that the royal governors had corrupted the colonial legislatures in the same way.

This destruction of the proper balance among different branches of government, they thought, led to tyranny. Consequently, it is not surprising that after their experience with the king and his royal governors, the Americans provided for very weak executive branches in most of the state constitutions. This, however, created other difficulties. The weak execu-

54

tive branches were not able to check the powers of the state legislatures. These legislatures passed laws that, in the opinion of many, violated basic rights, such as the right to property.

The problem that faced the Framers, then, was how to create a system of balanced government. They wanted to strengthen the executive branch without at the same time making it so strong that it could destroy the balance of power among the branches, as they believed the king and the royal governors had done.

The executive branch - Article II of the Constitution

The difficulty of organizing the executive branch raised the following questions which were dealt with by the Framers in the Constitution.

1. **Single or plural executive.** Should there be more than one chief executive?

The Framers easily agreed that there should be a single executive to avoid the possible problem of conflict between two leaders of equal power.

2. **Term of office.** How long should the chief executive remain in his position?

The Constitution sets the term of office at four years.

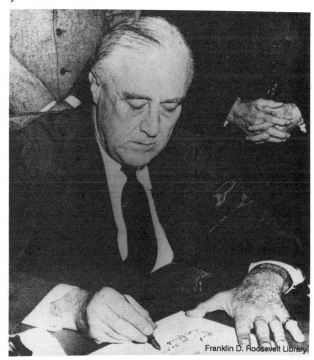

President Roosevelt signing the declaration of war against Japan, 1941

3. **Reelection.** Should the executive be eligible for reelection?

The Constitution originally set no limit upon the number of times a president could be reelected. However, the 22nd Amendment sets the limit at two terms.

4. **Powers.** What powers should be given to the executive branch of the government?

The executive branch was given those powers the Framers thought would be most efficiently carried out under the supervision of a single person, with the assistance of persons under his control. These include, for example, the responsibilities for (a) carrying out and enforcing laws made by Congress, (b) making treaties with foreign nations, and (c) conducting wars.

Although the Framers thought the executive branch should have enough power to fulfill its responsibilities, they also wanted to be sure it did not have too much power. They limited the powers of the executive branch by making it share most of its powers with Congress. This was intended to keep the powers balanced and to provide Congress with a way to check the use of power by the executive branch. This was accomplished in the following ways.

- Appointments. The power to appoint leading members of the executive branch was shared with Congress. The president had the right to nominate persons to fill these positions, but the Senate had the right to approve or disapprove of the persons nominated.

- Treaties. The power to make treaties with foreign nations was also shared with Congress. The president had the right to enter into a treaty with another nation, but the treaty had to be approved by the Senate.

- War. Although the president could conduct a war, only Congress had the power to declare war, and Congress controlled the money necessary to wage a war.

- Veto. Although the president could veto a law made by Congress, it could still become a law if two-thirds of Congress voted to override the veto.

- Impeachment. Finally, the Constitution gave the Congress the power to impeach the president. Only the House of Representatives could bring charges of impeachment. The

Senate had the responsibility of trying the president to determine guilt or innocence. If found guilty by two-thirds of the Senate, the president would be removed from office.

In spite of these details, if you look closely at Article II you will see that it is short and vague in comparison with Article I. It speaks of "executive power" but does not define it. Section 3 seems to give the president power to suggest legislation, which is not an executive power. Executive departments are mentioned, but there is no provision for creating them, deciding how many there should be, or how they should operate.

The Framers, never having experienced a democratically elected president, found it hard to imagine exactly what he would do. But they trusted George Washington, expected him to become the first president, and thought he could be counted upon to fill in the gaps and set wise examples that would be followed by later presidents. As we shall see, that is exactly what happened.

5. **Selection.** How should the president be selected?

The main alternatives debated by the Framers were to have the president selected by (a) the Congress, (b) the state legislatures, (c) the state governors, or (d) the people by direct election.

The Framers knew that whichever group had the right to select the president or replace him in a new election would have great power over him. This power might be used to benefit some groups at the expense of others. It also might make it difficult for the president to function properly. They also knew that if Congress was given the power to choose a president, then limiting him to one long term was a way to prevent his being manipulated by Congress in order to get reelected. If the president was not chosen by Congress, then providing for a shorter term would make him more accountable to the people and he might be permitted to run for reelection as many times as he wanted. The problem was given to a committee to develop a plan that a majority of the Framers would support.

The committee's plan was a clever compromise. It did not give any of the groups listed above the right to select the president. The plan showed that the Framers did not trust the people's judgment and knowledge. They thought the country was so large that it would be impossible for most people to be personally familiar with the candidates and their qualifications.

The plan gave "a little bit to everyone." It was very unusual. It created an organization called the electoral college which was given the responsibility of electing the president. The following describes the main parts of this plan.

- The electoral college would be organized once every four years to elect a president. After the election, it would be dissolved.

- Members of the electoral college, called electors, would be selected from all of the states. A state's number of electors would be the same as its number of representatives in Congress. The methods for selecting electors would be decided upon by the state legislatures.

- Each elector would vote for two people, one of whom could not be a resident of his state. This forced the state to vote for at least one person who might not represent its particular interests.

- The person who received a majority of votes in the electoral college would become president, and the person with the next largest number of votes would become vice president.

- If no one received a majority of the votes in the electoral college, then the House of Representatives would select the president by a majority vote, with each state having only one vote.

This compromise was quickly approved by the Framers. Although it was quite complicated and unusual, it seemed to them to be the solution to their problem. There was little doubt in the Framers' minds that George Washington would easily be elected the first president. However, there was great doubt among the Framers that anyone after Washington could ever get a majority vote in the electoral college. They left the convention believing that in almost all of the future elections for president the final decision would be made in the House of Representatives.

The electoral college is still in existence, although it functions quite differently from the way it did then.

The judicial branch - Article III of the Constitution

To complete the system of checks and balances, the Framers had to plan the judicial branch. They had fewer problems agreeing on how to organize the judiciary than they had with the other two branches.

Most of them already agreed about how courts should be organized and what responsibilities and powers they should be given. They created the Supreme Court as the head of the judicial branch and reached the following agreements.

- Judges should be independent of politics so that they could use their best judgment to decide cases and not be influenced by political pressures.

- The best way to make sure that judges would not be influenced by politics was to have them appointed, not elected, and to have them keep their positions "during good behavior." This meant that judges could not be removed from their positions unless they were impeached and convicted of "treason, bribery, or other crimes and misdemeanors."

There was also a good deal of agreement about the kinds of powers that the judicial branch should have. The judiciary was given the power to:

- decide conflicts between state governments, and

- decide conflicts that involved the national government.

And finally, they gave the Supreme Court the authority to handle two types of cases. These are:

- Cases in which the Supreme Court has original jurisdiction. These are cases which the Constitution says are not to be tried first in a lower court, but which are to go directly to the Supreme Court. Such cases involve a state government, a dispute between state governments, and cases involving ambassadors.

- Cases which have first been heard in lower courts and which are appealed to the Supreme Court. These are cases over which the Supreme Court has appellate jurisdiction.

Judicial review - an unanswered question

One important matter about the judicial branch was not decided by the Framers. This was whether the Supreme Court should be given the power of judicial review over the legislative and executive branches of the national government. To do so would be to give it the authority to declare acts of these branches of the national government unconstitutional. This would mean giving one branch of the national government the

power to ensure that the other branches did not exceed the limitations placed upon them by the Constitution, the higher law of the nation.

The power of judicial review had been given to the judicial branches of some of the state governments by their constitutions. Some of the Framers believed it was important to give this power to the judicial branch of the national government. This would be a way of making sure that the Congress and the president obeyed the limitations on their powers placed there by the Constitution. However, other Framers disagreed. They thought that it might be dangerous to give members of any branch of the government not elected by the people the power to strike down laws made by members of Congress, who were elected by the people.

Nothing specific was decided on this subject at the Convention. The only reference in the Constitution to the general powers of the Supreme Court is at the beginning of Article III. There you will find only the statement that the "judicial power of the United States, shall be vested in one supreme court, . . ."

The power of the Supreme Court to declare acts of the Congress and president unconstitutional was clearly established by the Supreme Court itself in 1803. You will learn more about the important subject of judicial review in a later lesson.

Reviewing and using the lesson

1. Why did most state constitutions provide for weak executive branches?

2. Explain three ways in which the Constitution requires the executive branch to share powers with the legislative branch. Why was this done?

3. What does the electoral college tell us about the Framers' opinion of the judgment and knowledge of the people?

4. Why did the Framers want federal judges to be independent of political pressures? How did they attempt to achieve this independence?

5. Explain what is meant by the power of judicial review.

6. What were some arguments for and against giving the Supreme Court the power of judicial review? What basic ideas that you have studied might be used in these arguments?

What conflicting opinions did the Framers have about the completed Constitution?

Purpose of Lesson 16

This lesson describes conflicting points of view of leading Framers about the Constitution. Most of the delegates argued for the adoption of the Constitution, though many had some reservations about it. The reservations of a few were so severe that they refused to sign the document. The position of one of these, George Mason, is explained in detail.

When you complete this lesson, you should be able to explain the position he took and give arguments in support of and in opposition to each of his major criticisms of the Constitution.

Framers for and against the Constitution

The following remarks were made by two of the Framers on the last day of the convention. One of these Framers signed the Constitution; the other did not. What do these comments tell you about the differences of opinion among the Framers concerning the Constitution they had developed and the problems they thought might arise in getting it approved?

> . . . every member [of the convention] should sign. A few characters of consequence, by opposing or even refusing to sign the Constitution, might do infinite mischief . . . . No man's ideas were more remote from the plan than [mine are] known to be; but is it possible to deliberate between anarchy . . . on one side, and the chance of good to be expected from the plan on the other? (Alexander Hamilton.)

> . . . a Civil war may result from the present crisis . . . . In Massachusetts . . . there are two parties, one devoted to Democracy, the worst . . . of all political evils, the other as violent in the opposite extreme . . . . for this and other reasons . . . the plan should have been proposed in a more mediating shape.

(Elbridge Gerry, 1744-1814, signer of the Declaration of Independence and 5th vice president of the United States.)

You can see from the opinions of the above writers that they must have expected strong opposition to the ratification of the Constitution. You have studied the major decisions made by the Framers. In the final weeks of the Convention, the only thing left to do was to put the plan they had agreed upon in written form. Accomplishing this meant getting agreement about how each section should be worded.

The delegates did not leave the convention thinking they had created a perfect government. The four months they had spent putting it together had been filled with strong disagreements. Some had walked out of the convention. Others refused to sign the finished document.

The government created by the Constitution was a great experiment in democracy. The delegates had used some old ideas about good government, such as representation, the separation of powers, and checks and balances. They had also developed some new ones, such as the electoral college. They had agreed on several important compromises in order to create a plan that a majority would accept.

Supporters and critics

This lesson focuses on the opinions of three of the delegates. Benjamin Franklin argued in support of the Constitution. George Mason argued against it. He was one of the three delegates remaining until the end of the convention who refused to sign the document. The final passage from James Madison's notes on the debates is also included. Read these selections and be prepared to answer the questions that follow.

Franklin's speech on the last day of the convention, September 17, 1787

The following speech was read by James Wilson, a fellow delegate from Pennsylvania, because

Franklin's age and illness made him too weak to deliver it himself.

> I confess that there are several parts of this Constitution which I do not at present approve . . . [But] the older I grow, the more apt I am to doubt my own judgement, and to pay more respect to the judgement of others. . . . In these sentiments . . . I agree with this Constitution with all its faults, if they are such; because I think a general Government necessary for us . . . [and] I doubt . . . whether any other Convention we can obtain, may be able to make a better Constitution. For when you assemble a number of men to have the advantage of their joint wisdom, you inevitably assemble with those men all their prejudices, their passions, their errors of opinion, their local interests, and their selfish views. From such an assembly can a perfect production be expected? It therefore astonishes me . . . to find this system approaching so near to perfection as it does . . . . Thus I consent . . . to this Constitution because I expect no better, and because I am not sure, that it is not the best . . . If every one of us in returning to our Constituents were to report the objections he has had to it . . . we might prevent its being generally received, and thereby lose all the salutary effects and great advantages resulting naturally in our favor among foreign Nations as well as among ourselves, from a real or apparent unanimity . . . . On the whole . . . I cannot help expressing a wish that every member of the Convention who may still have objections to it, would with me, on this occasion doubt a little of his own infallibility, and to make manifest our unanimity put his name to this instrument.

George Mason's objections to the Constitution

Less than a week before the convention ended, George Mason, the author of the Virginia Bill of Rights, wrote a list of objections on his copy of the draft of the Constitution. Some of the most important are set forth below.

1. The way members of the Senate are selected means that they are not representatives of the people or answerable to them. They have great powers such as the right to approve the appointment of ambassadors

and treaties recommended by the president, as well as the power to try the president and other members of government in cases of impeachment. These powers place the senators in such close connection with the president that together they will destroy any balance in the government and do whatever they please with the rights and liberties of the people.

2. The national judicial branch has been given so much power that it can destroy the judicial branches of the state governments by overruling them. If this were to happen and the only courts available were the federal courts, most people would not be able to afford to have their cases heard in these courts, and rich people would have an advantage that would enable them to oppress and ruin the poor.

3. The Constitution does not provide for a group of legislators to serve as advisers to the president. Such advisers have always been included in any safe and regular government. As a result, the president will not get proper advice, and will usually be advised by flattering and obedient favorites; or he will become a tool of the Senate.

4. The president of the United States has the unlimited power to grant pardons for treason. He may

sometimes use this power to protect people from punishment whom he has secretly encouraged to commit a crime, and in this way he can prevent the discovery of his own guilt.

5. The Constitution says that all treaties are the supreme law of the land. Since they can be made by the president with the approval of the Senate, together they have an exclusive legislative power in this area. This means they can act without the approval of the House of Representatives, the other branch of the legislature which is directly answerable to the people.

6. The Constitution only requires a majority vote in Congress to make all commercial and navigation laws instead of a two-thirds vote. But the economic interests of the five southern states are totally different from those of the eight northern states which have a majority of representatives in Congress. Requiring only a majority vote means Congress may make laws that will favor the merchants of the northern and eastern states at the expense of the agricultural interests of the southern states. This could ruin the economy of the southern states and leave people in poverty.

7. Since the Constitution gives Congress the power to make any laws it thinks are "necessary and proper" to carry out its responsibilities, there is no adequate limitation upon its powers. Congress could grant monopolies in trade and commerce, create new crimes, inflict unusual and severe punishments, and extend its powers as far as it wants. As a result, the powers of the state legislatures could be taken from them and Congress could dominate the entire nation.

George Mason had also made other criticisms of the Constitution during the convention. Some of them were accepted and some resulted in changes made after the convention. One of the most notable of his criticisms was that the Constitution did not contain a bill of rights. The story of how and why the Bill of Rights was added to the Constitution will be told in a following lesson.

Madison's last entry in his notes on the Constitution

The final entry that James Madison made in his notes on the convention describes the scene as the delegates were signing the document that they hoped would become the Constitution of the United States.

Whilst the last members were signing it, [Doctor] Franklin looking towards the Presi-

dent's Chair, at the back of which a rising sun happened to be painted, observed to a few members near him, that Painters had found it difficult to distinguish in their art a rising from a setting sun. [Franklin said] "I have often in the course of the Session looked at that behind the President without being able to tell whether it was rising or setting: But now at length I have the happiness to know that it is a rising and not a setting sun."

"Rising sun" chair used by Washington when he presided over the Philadelphia Convention

Reviewing and using the lesson

1. Describe Benjamin Franklin's attitude toward the Constitution. What reasons did he give for his view?

2. Explain each of George Mason's objections to the Constitution.

3. Select one of George Mason's objections and identify and describe an event in American history or a contemporary event that supports the objection.

4. Select one of George Mason's objections and explain what remedies our constitutional government provides for the type of problem he identified. Then, take and defend a position on whether or not the remedy is adequate.

What was the Federalists' position in the debate over ratification?

Purpose of Lesson 17

The people who supported ratification (approval) of the Constitution, which created a <u>federal government</u>, were called <u>Federalists</u>. Those who were against ratification of the Constitution were called <u>Anti-Federalists</u>. It is important to understand the differences between the opinions of these two groups. Many of the issues they raised are still being debated today. This lesson will help you understand the position of the Federalists. The next lesson will present the position of the Anti-Federalists.

When you complete this lesson, you should be able to explain the views of the Federalists and the following basic ideas and terms as used in this lesson.

Federalists
Anti-Federalists
ratifying conventions
The Federalist

The Federalists ask the voters to approve the Constitution

The Federalists knew that many members of Congress and the state governments were against the new Constitution, largely because it reduced state powers. So the Federalists decided <u>not</u> to ask the Congress or state governments to approve the Constitution, even though this is what they were expected to do.

James Madison developed the basic plan presented by the Federalists. The plan was to go directly to the <u>voters</u> to get them to approve the Constitution. The Constitution would be presented at special <u>ratifying conventions</u> to be held in each state. The delegates would be elected by popular vote of the people for the sole purpose of approving the Constitution. Madison's plan was consistent with the basic idea contained in the Preamble to the Constitution which says, "We the People . . . do ordain and establish this Constitution . . . . "

Another example of the social contract

The Federalists' plan was another example of the use of the idea of a social contract. The people who were to be governed by the new national government were asked to <u>consent</u> to its creation and to agree to obey its decisions. You may recognize this as the method for establishing a government set forth in the natural rights philosophy of John Locke and in the Declaration of Independence. In Jefferson's words, just governments "derive their . . . powers from the consent of the governed." Some people had argued, for example, that the Articles of Confederation were not valid or legitimate because they had never been presented to the people for their consent.

The Federalists attempt to act quickly to defeat the Anti-Federalists

The Framers at the convention approved this plan. They included a provision in the Constitution that would put it into effect after it had been ratified by the conventions of just nine of the thirteen states.

Once they had agreed upon their strategy, the Federalists encouraged their associates in the states to organize the state conventions and elect delegates to them as quickly as possible. They knew that the Anti-Federalists had not had much time to organize their opposition. By contrast, the Federalists had worked on the Constitution for almost four months. They knew the arguments for and against it and had organized themselves to get support for it. They thought that if the conventions acted quickly, the Anti-Federalists would have less time to organize opposition to ratification.

The struggle for ratification

But the Anti-Federalists put up a strong fight. The debates in the states over ratification took ten months. It was an intense and sometimes bitter political struggle. One of the most difficult fights for ratification was in the state of New York. To help the Federalist cause, three men--Alexander Hamilton, James Madison, and John Jay--were asked to write a series of articles to be published in a newspaper in New York. The articles were not intended to present all sides of the conflict over the Constitution. Their purpose was to convince people to support the ratification of the Constitution. These articles are now called *The Federalist*. They are considered to be the most important work written in defense of the new Constitution.

The men who wrote the Constitution were politicians. During the convention they had been engaged in serious conflicts of opinion. They had made compromises in developing the Constitution in order to get a majority of the delegates to vote for it. The compromises were also necessary to get people in the states to ratify the Constitution.

Alexander Hamilton, 1755 - 1804

The Federalists' arguments for the Constitution

In defending the new Constitution, the writers of *The Federalist* were very skilled at using the basic ideas about government which most Americans understood and accepted. They presented the Constitution as a well-organized, agreed-upon plan for the national government. The conflicts and compromises that had taken place during its development were downplayed in their attempt to present the Constitution as favorably as possible. The remainder of this lesson contains the main arguments that the Federalists made for their position.

Library of Congress

John Jay, 1745 - 1829

1. The civic virtue of the people cannot be relied upon alone to protect basic rights

Throughout history, the Federalists argued, the greatest dangers in republics to the common welfare and the natural rights of citizens had been from the selfish pursuit of their interests by groups of citizens who ignored the common welfare. Therefore, for almost two thousand years, political philosophers had insisted that republican government was only safe if the citizens possessed civic virtue. By civic virtue they meant that citizens had to be willing, when appropriate, to set aside their selfish interests if it was necessary to do so for the common welfare.

However, recent experiences with their state governments had led a number of people to doubt that they could rely upon the virtue of citizens to promote the common welfare and protect the rights of individuals. You will remember that many of the state legislatures had passed laws that helped people in debt at the expense of those to whom they owed money. These laws were seen by many as an infringement upon property rights which were, after all, one of the basic natural rights for which the Revolution had been fought in the first place.

If the proper working of a republican form of government could not rely upon the virtue of its citizens, what could it rely upon? How could a government be organized so it would not be dominated by self-interested individuals or factions at the expense of others?

2. The way the government is organized will protect basic rights

A major idea contained in *The Federalist* is that the national government set forth in the Constitution did not have to rely solely upon the civic virtue of the people to protect citizens' rights and promote their welfare. The writers believed that it was unrealistic to expect people in a large and diverse nation, living hundreds of miles apart, to be willing to give up their own interests for the benefit of others.

The Federalists argued that the rights and welfare of all would be protected by the complicated system of representation, separation of powers, and checks and balances provided by the Constitution. They also believed that the method of electing senators and presidents would increase the possibility that they would have the qualities required of good governing officials.

The Federalists took the position that the Constitution's strength was that it provided for different branches of government which would represent the different interests of the people. They also claimed that this complicated system would make it impossible for any individual or faction--or even a majority--to take complete control of the government to serve its selfish interests at the expense of the common welfare or the rights of individuals.

The large size of the nation, they argued, would make it particularly difficult for any one faction to attain a majority. Since so many interests and factions would be represented in the national government, it would be less likely that any one of them would dominate.

Some would argue that the system was so complicated that it would be difficult to get anything done, especially if one or more interested and powerful groups objected to something that was being planned. However, Madison, in *The Federalist*, clearly did not see this as a disadvantage. One of his criticisms of the state legislatures had been that they passed too many laws in the first place. Some of the Founders believed that the best way to prevent a bad law from being passed was to prevent a law from being passed at all.

3. The representation of different interests in the government will protect basic rights

The following are the branches among which the Constitution distributed the powers of the national government and the interests the Federalists argued each was supposed to represent.

a. Legislative branch. The House of Representatives would protect the people's local interests, since representatives would be chosen from small congressional districts. The Senate would protect the people's state interests, since it would be elected by state legislatures.

b. Executive branch. The president would protect the people's national interests, since he would be elected by a method that required electors to select him from among leaders who had achieved national prominence.

c. Judicial branch. The Supreme Court would protect the people's fundamental interests, since it was independent of political manipulation and therefore responsible only to the Constitution.

Did the national government have too much power?

The Federalists admitted that the new national government had much more power than the old national government, and that it had more control over the states. But they argued that it was a government limited to enumerated powers. The federal system and checks and balances ensured that those limits would not be violated. As a result, they claimed, the increased powers given to the government under the Constitution could only be used to protect, not to violate, the rights of the people.

Critics feared that giving so much power to a national government might be a serious threat to their rights and welfare. The arguments of these people, the Anti-Federalists, is the subject of the next lesson.

Reviewing and using the lesson

1. Who were the Federalists? Who were the Anti-Federalists?

2. Why was *The Federalist* written? Who wrote the articles?

3. Why didn't the Federalists want the Constitution submitted to the existing Congress or state governments for ratification?

4. According to the Federalists, where did the greatest dangers to the rights of citizens come from? What evidence had there been in their recent experience that supported this position?

5. Explain the opinion that civic virtue was needed to make a republican form of government work properly.

6. Why did the Federalists think they could not rely just upon civic virtue to make the new nation work properly?

7. How did the Federalists think they could make republican government work properly in a large and diverse nation?

8. How did the Federalists answer the criticism that the Constitution gave the federal government too much power?

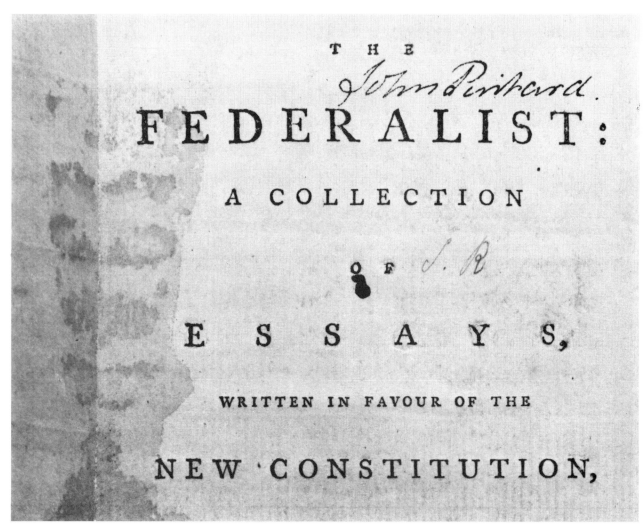

Courtesy of The New-York Historical Society, New York City

Title page of The Federalist

What was the Anti-Federalists' position in the debate over ratification?

Courtesy, Museum of Fine Arts, Boston

Mercy Otis Warren, 1728 - 1814

Purpose of Lesson 18

In this lesson you will learn the position of the Anti-Federalists. To understand their point of view, we will focus upon the writings of Mercy Otis Warren, the author of many plays and political pamphlets. The Anti-Federalists' position was based mainly on the ideas that had been discussed for over two thousand years about the kind of society that was necessary for a republic. You will also learn of one of the greatest contributions to our Constitution that resulted from the debate between the Federalists and Anti-Federalists--the Bill of Rights.

When you finish this lesson you should be able to explain the arguments of the Anti-Federalists, and the response of the Federalists to these arguments.

The concerns of the Anti-Federalists

Most Americans were very suspicious of government, but the Anti-Federalists were especially mistrustful of government in general and strong national government in particular. This mistrust was the basis of their opposition to the Constitution which they feared had created a government the people could not control.

The importance of representative government and civic virtue

In general, the Anti-Federalists were older Americans who had grown up believing in the basic ideas of republicanism. These included the idea that in a republic, the greatest power should be placed in a legislature composed of representatives elected by the people of a community. It had always been thought that this kind of representative government would only work in a small community of citizens with similar interests and beliefs, because in such a community it would be easier for people to agree upon what was in their common welfare.

In addition, it was widely believed that people living in small agrarian communities would be more likely to possess the civic virtue required of republican citizens. Living closely together they would be more likely to be willing to set aside their own selfish interests when necessary and to work together for their common welfare.

The Anti-Federalists understood that the Federalists were proposing a government that was the opposite of this type of republican government. It was large and powerful, it included numerous diverse communities, and its capital would be far away from most of the people it represented. The Anti-Federalists believed such a system would inevitably pose a threat to the rights of the people.

Many distinguished Americans were Anti-Federalists. George Mason, whose arguments you read in Lesson 16 of this unit, was one. Other prominent Anti-Federalists included Patrick Henry, Luther Martin, Robert Yates, and George Clinton.

Patrick Henry, 1736 - 1799

The arguments of the Anti-Federalists

Mercy Otis Warren was a playwright as well as an Anti-Federalist writer. She is noteworthy because of her unusual ability to enter the man's world of early American politics. Her main criticisms of the Constitution are a good example of the Anti-Federalist position. The Anti-Federalists argued that the Constitution had the following flaws.

- It gave too much power to the national government at the expense of the powers of the state governments.

- It gave too much power to the executive branch of the national government at the expense of the other branches.

- It gave Congress too much power because of the "necessary and proper clause."

- It did not adequately separate the powers of the executive and legislative branch.

- It allowed the national government to keep an army during peacetime.

- It did not include a bill of rights.

- It should have been developed in meetings whose proceedings were open to the public.

The fear of a strong national government

Warren and the other Anti-Federalists feared that, because of the flaws they believed the Constitution contained, the new national government would be a threat to their natural rights. They also thought that the Constitution had been developed by an elite and privileged group to create a national government for the purpose of serving its own selfish interests. She and most of the Anti-Federalists thought that the only safe government was one that was (a) local and closely linked with the will of the people, and (b) controlled by the people, by such means as yearly elections, and by replacing people in key positions often.

The Federalists' response

The Anti-Federalists had some of the traditional arguments on their side about what made a good government. However, the Federalists were better organized. The Constitution and their arguments to support it contained a solution for the problem of creating a republican government in a large and diverse nation. They were able to convince a large number of people to support their position by the following arguments.

- The civic virtue of the people could no longer be relied upon as the sole support of a government that would protect the people's rights and promote their welfare.

- The way in which the Constitution organized the government, including the separation of powers and checks and balances, was the best way to promote the goals of republicanism.

- A strong national government was needed to deal with the economic and other problems of the new nation.

The agreement to add a bill of rights

By June of 1788, nine states had voted to ratify the Constitution. But the important states of New York and Virginia had not yet approved the Constitution. The debates were very close in these states because of the fear of creating such a large and powerful national government. Finally, the people of New York and Virginia voted in favor of the Constitution. However, this did not happen until the Federalists promised that one of the first things the new national government would do would be to adopt a <u>bill of rights</u> that would place further limitations on the powers of the national government. That promise reduced much of the support for the Anti-Federalists.

The Federalists had argued against adding a bill of rights to the Constitution. They claimed that the way the government was organized made it impossible for it to violate people's rights. Some argued that adding a bill of rights would not prevent a government from violating people's rights if it wanted to. Most of the state constitutions had bills of rights and many of those governments were thought to have violated at least some of the people's rights anyway. Some Federalists even argued that a national bill of rights might be a dangerous idea, since it might give the impression that the people only expected protection of those rights that were listed.

Finally, a compromise was reached. In order to get some of the Anti-Federalists to support the Constitution, the Federalists agreed that when the first Congress was held, it would draft a bill of rights to be added to the Constitution. It was to list those rights of citizens which were not to be violated by the <u>federal</u> government. But they insisted that the bill of rights include a statement saying that the list of rights should not be interpreted to mean that they were the only rights the people had.

The Federalists deserve the credit for writing the Constitution, which created our present form of government. The debate resulting from the Anti-Federalists' objections to the Constitution resulted in the addition of the Bill of Rights. It was not a useless addition. The Bill of Rights has proved to be vitally important to the protection of the basic rights of the American people.

Reviewing and using the lesson

1. Why did the Anti-Federalists believe that the Constitution would not be able to maintain a system of republican government?

2. List specific objections to the Constitution that Anti-Federalists made.

3. What does the following quotation tell you about a major fear of the Anti-Federalists?

> We ought to consider the depravity of human nature, the predominant thirst for power which is in the breast of everyone, the temptation rulers may have, and the unlimited confidence placed in them by this system. (A participant in the North Carolina debates over the ratification of the Constitution.)

4. The Anti-Federalists lost their battle to prevent the adoption of the Constitution. However, they left a permanent impact on the Constitution. How?

5. Would you have voted to ratify the Constitution as written in 1787? Why?

Unit Four: Establishment of the Government

Purpose of Unit Four

As you have learned, the Constitution was ratified in 1788. But having a constitution doesn't mean you have a government. The Constitution was a plan for creating and operating the new government, much like an architect's plan for building a house. It described the way the government was to be organized, its powers, and its limitations. It is important to understand that the Framers had purposely written the Constitution as a general framework for the government. They had left out many details they knew would have to be added by future presidents and members of Congress. This unit will provide you with an understanding of how the government was organized under the Constitution. It will also tell you about some of the unexpected developments that have had a significant influence on the way our nation is governed today.

How was the Constitution used to organize the new government?

Washington being sworn in

Purpose of Lesson 19

This lesson explains the steps taken by the new Congress to draft the Bill of Rights and to organize the executive and judicial branches.

When you have completed this lesson, you should be able to explain why the Bill of Rights was added as a series of amendments to the Constitution and why it applied only to actions by the federal government. You should also be able to explain how the federal court system and executive branch were organized. When you finish this lesson you should be familiar with the following terms.

Ninth Amendment
Tenth Amendment
Judiciary Act of 1789
federal district court
appellate court
president's cabinet
bureaucracy

Tasks of the first Congress

The newly elected senators and representatives of the First Congress met in New York in April of 1789 to begin their work. Four of the tasks they had to accomplish are listed below.

1. Name the new president and vice president
2. Draft a bill of rights
3. Organize the judicial branch of government
4. Organize the executive branch of government

The following briefly describes how Congress, using the guidelines given to it in the Constitution, accomplished these tasks.

1. Naming the new president and vice president

Article II of the Constitution deals with the executive branch of the federal government. Section 1 of that article sets forth the way the president and vice president are to be chosen by electors appointed by the state legislatures. Once all of the ballots are collected, the president of the Senate is to supervise the counting of the ballots to see who has been elected. When this was done in 1789, the votes showed, as expected, that George Washington had been elected president. John Adams, with the second highest number of votes, became vice president.

2. Drafting the Bill of Rights

In his inaugural address, George Washington urged the Congress to respond to the widespread demand to add a bill of rights to the Constitution.

As you have read, during the struggle to get the states to ratify the Constitution, it had been criticized for not having a bill of rights. To answer this objection, the Federalists had agreed to the addition of a bill of rights as soon as the new government was established.

When the first Congress met, James Madison wanted to fulfill this promise. He recommended that the new Constitution be <u>rewritten</u> to include a number of limitations on the powers of the government.

These limitations would protect certain basic rights of the people. He suggested placing most of these limits in Article I of the Constitution following Section 9, where there were already a number of limitations on the powers of Congress.

Madison also was persuaded by his friend Thomas Jefferson that the people were entitled to such a "declaration of rights against every government." He believed that this was especially true for some important rights which he thought the Constitution should protect not only from the federal government but from state governments as well. These were the rights to freedom of religion and expression and the right to a trial by jury in criminal cases.

Roger Sherman of Connecticut objected to making changes in the body of the Constitution itself. He argued that since the Constitution had just been ratified, it should not be rewritten. He said that any changes or additions should be listed as amendments at the end of the Constitution. A majority of both the House of Representatives and the Senate agreed, and the Bill of Rights was added at the end of the Constitution as a series of amendments, approved by Congress, and later ratified by the necessary eleven states on December 15, 1791.

The Bill of Rights contains ten amendments. The first eight list basic protections that had already been guaranteed in most of the state constitutions. These include freedom of religion, press, speech, assembly, and trial by jury. The Ninth Amendment states that the listing of certain rights does not mean that these are the only rights the people have. Finally, the Tenth Amendment states that the powers not given to the federal government by the Constitution, nor prohibited by the Constitution to the states, are to be retained by the states and the people.

In drafting the Bill of Rights, Congress rejected Madison's proposal that some of its basic rights be protected from the powers of state governments as well as the federal government. A decision of the Supreme Court in 1833 (*Barron v. Baltimore*) made clear that the Bill of Rights only applied to the federal government. However, today most of the protections of the Bill of Rights have been applied to the states through the Supreme Court's interpretations of the 14th Amendment. Since the Bill of Rights has been so important in the history of the United States, a number of lessons will be devoted to it later in this text.

3. Organizing the judicial branch

Article III of the Constitution says that "the judicial power of the United States, shall be vested in one supreme court, and in such inferior courts as the Congress may from time to time . . . establish." As you can see, the Framers had written only this very general guideline and given the first Congress the task of organizing a system of federal courts.

Congress did this by passing a law known as the Judiciary Act of 1789. It established two levels of federal courts below the Supreme Court.

- The first level included a federal district court in each state. These federal courts were responsible for the first hearing or trial of most cases involving the Constitution and federal laws.

- The second level was a system of appellate courts. These were courts where decisions made by the federal district court in each state could be reviewed for errors of law. From these appellate courts, cases could be appealed to the Supreme Court, the highest court in the federal system.

In addition to the system of federal courts established by the Constitution and Congress to rule on federal law, each state had its own courts established by its own legislature to rule on state law. This system of federal and state courts is organized in much the same way today as it was when the nation was founded. (see chart on page 71)

Today the Supreme Court plays an important role in our federal government. However, during these early years, the Supreme Court played a much less significant role. The first Chief Justice, John Jay, spent little time on the job. While he was serving as Chief Justice, he spent a year in England on a diplomatic mission and ran for governor of New York twice. Another of the first justices, John Rutledge, did not attend a single session of the Supreme Court during its first two years. Oliver Ellsworth, the next Chief Justice, resigned his position in 1800. The Supreme Court was not considered an important branch of the federal government at that time. We will learn of the growth of the power and importance of the Court in later lessons.

THE UNITED STATES COURT SYSTEM

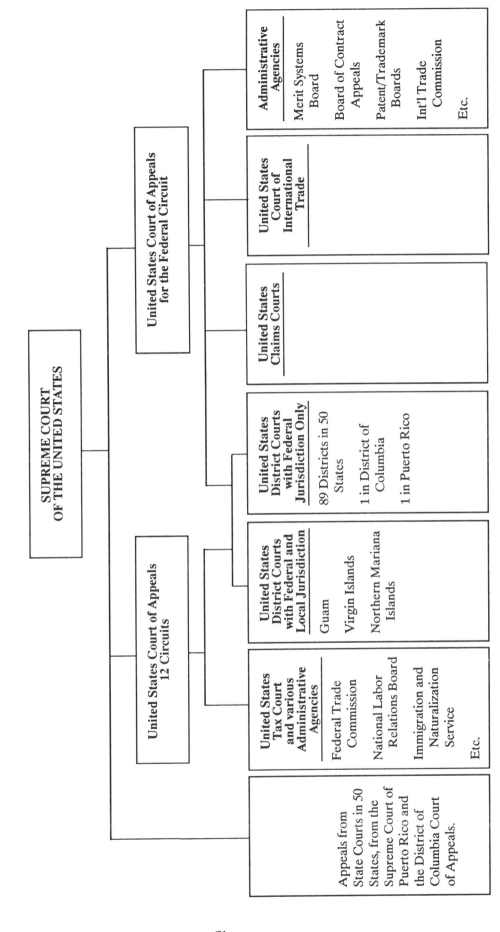

SUPREME COURT OF THE UNITED STATES

United States Court of Appeals 12 Circuits

United States Court of Appeals for the Federal Circuit

United States Tax Court and various Administrative Agencies

Federal Trade Commission

National Labor Relations Board

Immigration and Naturalization Service

Etc.

United States District Courts with Federal and Local Jurisdiction

Guam

Virgin Islands

Northern Mariana Islands

United States District Courts with Federal Jurisdiction Only

89 Districts in 50 States

1 in District of Columbia

1 in Puerto Rico

United States Claims Courts

United States Court of International Trade

Administrative Agencies

Merit Systems Board

Board of Contract Appeals

Patent/Trademark Boards

Int'l Trade Commission

Etc.

Appeals from State Courts in 50 States, from the Supreme Court of Puerto Rico and the District of Columbia Court of Appeals.

71

Washington and his cabinet

4. Organizing the executive branch

The Constitution gives Congress the power to organize the executive branch. When the first Congress met, its members were still concerned about the need to control the executive branch and to prevent the president from gaining too much power. This concern was made clear in the debate over how the president should be addressed. It was first proposed that he should be referred to or introduced as "His Highness, the President of the United States of America." However, since the government was a republic and not a monarchy ruled by a king, they decided that this would not be proper. Instead, Congress agreed on the simpler, more democratic form of "The President of the United States."

The first Congress began to organize the executive branch by creating a number of departments to be under the control of the president to help fulfill the responsibilities of the presidency. The persons to be in charge of these departments were to be called "secretaries." These positions were very important under President Washington since he used the heads of these departments as his advisers. Together, they became the president's "cabinet." The first of these departments and their secretaries were the following:

- Thomas Jefferson, Secretary of State, who was responsible for handling relations with other nations

- Henry Knox, Secretary of War, who was responsible for handling defense

- Alexander Hamilton, Secretary of the Treasury, who was responsible for handling the financial affairs of the federal government

In addition to these three, Edmund Randolph was selected to be the attorney general. It was his responsibility to handle all Supreme Court cases involving the federal government, and to give advice on legal questions to the president and other members of the executive branch.

The present organization of the executive branch

Of course, today the organization of the executive branch of the federal government is far more complex than during the early years of this nation. When Jefferson was president, there were only 2,120 people working in this branch and it had only three departments. There are now more than 3 million people working in the executive branch, and it has thirteen

The Executive Branch

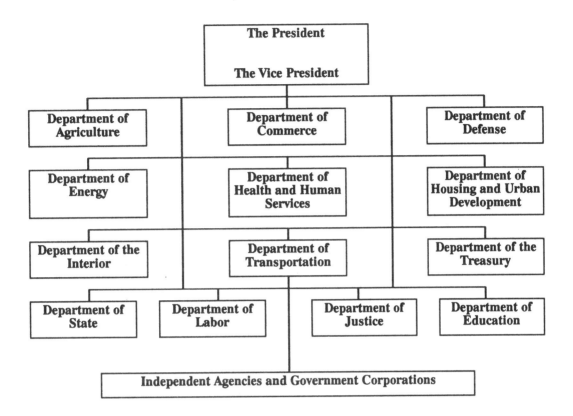

departments and numerous other federal agencies. Today there are more people working in the executive branch of the federal government than there were in the entire nation at the time of the first government.

The Constitution does not mention a federal bureaucracy and the Founders had no idea that the executive branch would grow to be so large and have so many responsibilities. However, the framework for government set up by the Constitution has been able to deal with these developments as well as the unforeseen appearance of political parties, which is discussed in the next lesson. To get a better understanding of the structure of the executive branch of the federal government today, look at the simplified organizational chart above.

Reviewing and using the lesson

1. How was a Bill of Rights included in the Constitution? What rights are included in it? Do citizens have rights not specified in the Bill of Rights?

2. It was the task of the first Congress elected under the Constitution to organize the executive and judicial branches of government, which were only described in general terms in the Constitution. Briefly describe how this was done.

3. The executive branch of the federal government has grown tremendously since 1789. What historical events and trends may account for this? What dangers, if any, are there in such growth?

4. The idea of having one person to serve as president and lead the executive branch was developed when our nation had less than three million people. Today our nation has over 240 million people and is a world power. Is it still reasonable to have one person serve as the head of the executive branch? Might it be more efficient, for example, to have two people--one for domestic and one for foreign policy? Why? Develop and explain the strengths and weaknesses of other alternatives for leadership in the executive branch.

What caused the rise of political parties?

Collection of the Boatmen's National Bank of St. Louis

Voting in a county election in the early 19th century

Purpose of Lesson 20

You have learned that the Framers did not foresee the growth of the executive branch of government or the establishment of the large federal bureaucracy we have today. The Constitution they had written, however, did allow for these events as the need arose. Soon after the government was established, there was another unforeseen development that the Framers did not provide for and which they were very much against. This was the formation of political parties such as the Democratic and Republican parties we have today. This lesson will describe how political parties came to be formed and their importance to our present system.

When you complete the lesson, you should be able to explain the opposing points of view which led to the development of political parties, and the significance of the following ideas and terms as they are used in this lesson.

faction
political parties
Federalist Party
Republican Party
general welfare clause
necessary and proper clause
Alien and Sedition Acts
election of 1800

Why the Framers were against political parties

James Madison had argued in *The Federalist* that one of the Constitution's major advantages was its organization of the government in such a way that factions would be controlled. He defined a faction as a group of citizens, either a majority or a minority, that pursues its own selfish interests at the expense of other citizens' interests or the common welfare. As you have learned, many of the Framers believed that factions were dangerous for republican government for this very reason.

In the minds of the Framers, political parties were factions. If political parties became a part of government, each would fight to promote the interests of its own members without regard for the common welfare. The government would then be controlled by, and serve the interests of, the strongest political party and not promote justice or protect the rights of any groups that might be in the minority.

The Framers believed that people had a natural tendency to differ in their opinions and to join together with others whose opinions were similar to theirs. They also believed that one of the purposes of government was to protect the individual's rights to property. And, because of differences in abilities, experiences, opportunities, and interests, some people would inevitably have more property than others. This and other differences would naturally lead to people's dividing into different factions with different interests.

However, Madison argued that the influence of these factions would be limited by the complicated system of government planned in the Constitution. Because of its complexity and the size and diversity of the nation, he argued, it would be impossible for any one or more of these factions to form a majority which could control the government in its own interests. In spite of this system, however, political parties did develop and are now an accepted part of the American political system.

Conflicting ideas lead to the development of political parties

When George Washington was first serving as president, he wanted to be able to get advice from people whose opinions he most valued. He had two such persons in his cabinet, Jefferson and Hamilton. They had very different ideas about what the government's policies should be, and they were often in conflict. After a while, when Washington began to accept Hamilton's opinion in most matters, Jefferson resigned from the cabinet. During this period, Hamilton and his followers became known as the Federalists, and Jefferson and his followers became known as the Republicans. (This is the origin of the Democratic Party of today, not the Republican Party.) Since the differences of opinions between these groups played a large part in the development of political parties in the United States, they are worth studying.

The Republicans disagree with the Federalists

Jefferson had supported the ratification of the Constitution, but he and his followers were still concerned about it. They thought that the description of the powers of the federal government contained in the Constitution was so general and so vague that the government would be able to do almost anything it wished. The Republicans believed strongly in small, local government. They said that to place so much power in the federal government would be a threat to the rights of the people. Further, such power violated a basic principle of republicanism. This principle required small communities of citizens whose interests were similar enough for them to agree upon what was best for their common welfare.

The Federalists disagree with the Republicans

The Federalists disagreed. They said that the federal government could not overpower the state governments because its powers had been delegated to it by the people. The people had the right to reduce or eliminate the powers of the federal government by amending the Constitution. They also said that the federal government had only been given those powers that were enumerated, or listed, in the Constitution. And this listing was an adequate limitation upon its powers.

Jefferson's concern over the interpretation of the Constitution

No part of the Constitution did more to raise the fears of Jefferson and his followers than Article I, Section 8, which sets forth the powers of Congress. Although it does seem to limit Congress by clearly listing a number of its responsibilities and powers, it also contains two clauses which are very general. These are the general welfare and the necessary and proper clauses. These clauses read:

The Congress shall have power:

- to lay and collect taxes . . . to pay the debts and provide for the common defence and general welfare of the United States . . .

- to make all laws which shall be necessary and proper for carrying into execution the foregoing powers, [the powers given to Congress under Section 8].

Problem solving

How well do you understand Jefferson's concern?

Suppose you gave the members of your student government the power to make whatever rules for your school they thought were "necessary and proper" for your "general welfare."

- Who would be in the position to decide what was "necessary and proper"?

- Who would decide what the "general welfare" was?

- What limitations would there be on their powers?

Conflicts between the Federalists and the Republicans

The differences in political philosophy between Hamilton and Jefferson led them to disagree greatly on a number of specific issues regarding how the new government should be run. The following are three of the major issues on which they took opposing sides.

1. The establishment of the Bank of the United States

As Secretary of the Treasury, Hamilton had wanted to demonstrate the power he believed the federal government had and to strengthen the new nation's weak economy. To achieve these goals he made a number of recommendations to the Congress. One was that it pass a law establishing the Bank of the United States. Congress passed the law. This aroused much controversy.

Here we will consider the constitutional argument over whether Article I, Section 8 of the Constitution gave Congress the power to pass such a law. Hamilton said that it did; Jefferson said that it did not.

Hamilton said that the creation of the Bank was a "necessary and proper" method of carrying out the responsibilities given to Congress by the Constitution, such as collecting taxes and regulating trade.

Jefferson replied that the "necessary and proper" clause should be interpreted as if it read "absolutely and indispensably necessary." Clearly, this interpre-

Bank of the United States   Library of Congress

tation would have severely limited the power of the Congress. Certainly, the creation of the Bank would not have passed this restrictive test. Jefferson understood this, and this was exactly what he intended.

President Washington accepted Hamilton's position. He signed the legislation establishing the Bank of the United States. Thus, a large step was taken toward increasing the power of the federal government.

2. Foreign relations

In 1793, war broke out between the French and the English. The Federalists and the Republicans disagreed on what the United States should do. The Federalists wanted the United States to help the English since there was more trade between the Americans and the English than with the French. They also opposed the radicalism of the French Revolution. The Republicans wanted the United States to help the French, because they had helped the Americans fight the English during the Revolutionary War. They also supported the French because they were fighting their own revolution against the French monarchy.

Washington tried to prevent the people from dividing into opposing camps over this issue. He declared that the United States was neutral and would not take sides in the war. When he left office after his second term, he warned the country against entering into permanent alliances with foreign governments. He also warned the American people to beware of the presence of dangerous "faction" and of the harmful effects of political parties.

3. The Alien and Sedition Acts

In the election of 1796, John Adams, a Federalist, became president. But Thomas Jefferson, a Republican, was elected vice president. This increased the conflict between the Federalists and the Republicans.

Jefferson and his followers criticized the way Adams and the Federalists in Congress were running the government. Adams and the Federalist majority in Congress were able to get laws passed called the Alien and Sedition Acts. These laws gave the president the power to force foreigners to leave the country if he considered them dangerous. They also made it a crime to say malicious and untrue things about the government.

Jefferson and the other Republicans were outraged at the laws and at their enforcement by Federalist judges. They knew the laws were intended to keep them from criticizing the government. James Madison joined with Thomas Jefferson to write the "Kentucky and Virginia Resolutions." They claimed that the states had a right to decide if the federal government had exceeded its powers. These resolutions would have given the state legislatures the power to declare laws made by the Congress, such as the Alien and Sedition Acts, null and void. The resolutions were not accepted by the other states. If they had been, they would have given the states a large amount of power over the federal government.

Jefferson is elected president

In the presidential election of 1800, Aaron Burr and Thomas Jefferson each received the same number of electoral votes. As a result, the selection of the president had to be made, as stated in the Constitution, by the House of Representatives. Jefferson was elected president.

The election of 1800 was of great importance to the new government. Although the Federalists were unhappy that they had lost, they accepted it and turned over control of the federal government to the Republicans. For the first time in modern history, the control of a government was given to new leaders as the result of a democratic election rather than by hereditary succession or the violent overthrow of a government.

After the War of 1812, the Federalist Party was no longer significant in American politics. The Federalists tended to be suspicious of democracy and distrustful of the people. The mood of the country, however, was becoming increasingly democratic. In the face of this growing spirit of equality and steps to lower or eliminate property qualifications for voting, the Federalists could not compete with the Republicans who more accurately represented the beliefs and opinions of the common people.

Political parties today

Political parties are now an accepted and valued part of the American political system. Many people argue that as the nation became more democratic, political parties were inevitable. Political parties serve several important purposes. They provide people with a way to organize support for candidates for public office. Also, they are a means of persuading more people to vote. By joining or supporting a political party, people show their support or opposition to the policies of whatever party is in power. As a result, political parties are seen as an important means of making sure that the political authority of the government is in fact derived from the people. And, finally, the presence of at least two parties is thought to be essential if the governed are to have a genuine choice.

Reviewing and using the lesson

1. Why did the Framers think political parties were dangerous in a republican form of government? How had they hoped to prevent political parties?

2. What were the first two political parties? What different points of view led to their formation?

3. Explain why Thomas Jefferson distrusted the "necessary and proper" clause of the Constitution? Do you agree with Jefferson's fear? Why?

4. Why do you think President Washington's acceptance of Alexander Hamilton's interpretation of the "necessary and proper" clause, which would allow for a Bank of the United States, was a large step toward increasing the power of the federal government?

5. Do you agree with Madison's and Jefferson's response to the Alien and Sedition Acts? If it had been accepted, what effect would it have had on our system of government?

6. What advantages do political parties have in a democratic system of government? What might be some of their disadvantages?

What is judicial review and why is it controversial?

The Supreme Court of the United States, 1987

Purpose of Lesson 21

Judicial review is the power of the judicial branch of a government to declare acts of the legislative and executive branches to be in violation of the government's constitution. When a court makes such a decision, it orders that the decision made by the other part of the government be considered "null and void" which means that it is not to be obeyed or enforced. In the United States, the federal judiciary, headed by the Supreme Court, now has this power over all parts of our government. State courts have this power over other branches of state governments.

Throughout our history, there have been great differences of opinion about whether the judicial branch should have this power and how it should be used. The controversy raises basic questions about representative government and majority rule on the one hand, and constitutional government and the protection of basic rights and unpopular minorities on the other hand.

This lesson and the next will explain how the Supreme Court gained the power of judicial review

and help you understand the continuing controversies that have resulted from its having this power.

When you finish this lesson, you should be able to explain the different positions regarding judicial review and its role in a constitutional democracy. You should also be able to describe the issues raised and the argument of the Supreme Court in the case of *Marbury v. Madison*. The following ideas and terms are contained in this lesson.

> **null and void**
> **judicial review**
> **unconstitutional**
> **supremacy clause**
> **writ of mandamus**
> **Marbury v. Madison**

Should the Supreme Court have the power to declare acts of the president and Congress unconstitutional?

One of the new ideas about government that developed in this nation was the idea that the

78

Supreme Court and lower courts in the judicial branch should have the power to interpret the Constitution and decide what it means. In some situations, this means that the Supreme Court will order that a law passed by a majority in Congress or in a state legislature violates the Constitution and therefore is not to be obeyed or enforced.

Problem solving

Do you think the Supreme Court should have the power of judicial review?

Suppose you could step back in time to decide whether the Supreme Court should be given the power of judicial review over acts of Congress. Study the choices below, the results of each, and be prepared to take and defend a position in favor of one of the alternatives.

Choice 1. Give the Supreme Court the power to declare laws passed by Congress unconstitutional.

Result. The Supreme Court would have the power to order that a law that had been passed by a majority of representatives in Congress, who were elected by citizens to represent their interests, should not be obeyed or enforced.

Choice 2. Deny the Supreme Court the power to declare laws passed by Congress unconstitutional.

Result. This would mean that all laws passed by a majority of representatives in Congress must be obeyed and enforced.

In order to develop and defend your decision, consider the following questions.

1. Does your choice conflict with the principles of representative government and majority rule? If so, how?

2. Is your choice more democratic? If so, how?

3. Might your choice place basic rights at the mercy of temporary emotions and current popularity?

4. Might your choice result in the majority tyrannizing the minority? If so, how?

How did the Supreme Court get the power of judicial review?

If you read the Constitution, you will not find any mention of the power of judicial review. As you will see, however, soon after the beginning of the new government, the Constitution was interpreted to give the Supreme Court this power.

Judicial review under British and state governments

The Founders were familiar with the idea that some part of government should be given the power to decide whether activities of the other parts of government had violated the "higher law" of a nation. Under British rule, the Privy Council, a group which advised the king, had the power to overrule decisions made by colonial courts if they violated English laws. Following the Revolution, some state constitutions gave this power to the judicial branches of their governments. Even though the belief in legislative supremacy was strong, several state courts had declared laws made by their legislatures to be unconstitutional.

The Supreme Court gains the power of judicial review over state governments

The Framers of the Constitution wanted to correct a basic weakness in the national government under the Articles of Confederation. As you have learned, under the Articles, the states had the right to decide whether or not they would obey and enforce the laws of the national government. To strengthen the new government, the Framers wrote Article VI, which, in part, reads:

> *This constitution, and the laws of the United States which shall be made in pursuance thereof; and all treaties made . . . under the authority of the United States, shall be the supreme law of the land; and the judges in every state shall be bound thereby, anything in the constitution or laws of any state to the contrary notwithstanding.*

As you have learned, this section of the Constitution is known as the supremacy clause. It has been interpreted to mean that the Supreme Court can order that state laws not be enforced if they violate federal laws or the Constitution. The First Congress also made this power clear in the Judiciary Act of 1789.

The Supreme Court first used its power of judicial review over state governments in 1796. After the Revolutionary War, the United States had signed a peace treaty with the British that said all debts owed by

Americans to English citizens would be paid. However, the state of Virginia had passed a law which cancelled all debts owed by Virginians to British citizens. Since this law clearly violated the peace treaty, the Supreme Court ruled that the law could not be enforced because the laws and treaties of the federal government are the supreme law of the land. As a result, citizens of Virginia were responsible for paying their debts.

The Supreme Court establishes its power of judicial review over Congress

The question of whether the Supreme Court should have the power of judicial review over the legislative and executive branches of the federal government was discussed during the Philadelphia Convention and the debates over ratification. But, no decision was made that clearly gave the Court this power. However, many historians believe that a majority of the Framers supported this idea. Some of the Framers assumed that the Court would have this power. Alexander Hamilton, for example, made this assumption in *The Federalist.*

The story of how the Supreme Court established its power of judicial review over the other branches of the federal government involves one of the most famous cases in our history, the case of *Marbury v. Madison*, which was decided in 1803. The following describes this case and its results.

The case of Marbury v. Madison

After Thomas Jefferson defeated the Federalist president, John Adams, in the election of 1800, Adams had several weeks remaining in office. During this time, Adams wanted to make sure that the Federalists would continue to influence the government long after Jefferson and the Republicans took over. The Federalists, who controlled Congress, passed a new judiciary act creating a number of new federal courts. Adams filled the new positions on these courts with Federalists. He also appointed his secretary of state, John Marshall, to be the Chief Justice of the United States.

When Thomas Jefferson became president, some of the documents which officially gave a number of Federalists their new jobs as judges had not been delivered to them. John Marshall had apparently forgotten to do this in his last days as Secretary of State before taking the position of Chief Justice. Jefferson did not want more Federalists serving as judges, so he ordered the new Secretary of State, James Madison, not to deliver the documents.

President Adams had appointed William Marbury to serve as justice of the peace for the District of Columbia. Marbury wanted the job and was upset with Jefferson's decision not to give it to him. He tried to find a way to get what he believed was rightfully his. He discovered that the Judiciary Act of 1789 gave the Supreme Court the power of writ of mandamus. A writ of mandamus is a court order that forces an officer of the government to do something that person is supposed to do, such as, in this case, deliver the documents that had been officially approved.

Marbury knew that John Marshall, a Federalist, was now Chief Justice, and he believed Marshall would be sympathetic with his situation. He decided that the best way to get his new position was to ask the Supreme Court to issue a writ of mandamus ordering Madison to deliver the document.

This put Chief Justice Marshall in a difficult position. He was worried about what might happen if he ordered Madison to deliver Marbury's document and President Jefferson ordered him not to, as he had threatened to do. Courts must rely on the executive branch for the enforcement of the laws. If Jefferson were to refuse to obey the decision of the Supreme Court, it would make the Court appear weak and powerless. However, if the Supreme Court did not order the President to deliver the document, the Court would also look weak.

The major issues in Marbury v. Madison

Chief Justice Marshall was faced with a difficult problem. He thought of a remarkable solution that let him avoid a confrontation with the President and, at the same time, establish the Supreme Court's power of judicial review. In arriving at this solution, Marshall asked three key questions.

1. Does Marbury have a right to the appointment?

2. If Marbury has a right to the appointment and his right has been violated, do the laws of the country give him a way to have things set right?

3. If the laws of the country give Marbury a way to deal with this problem, is that way a writ of mandamus from the Supreme Court?

Marshall's Decision

Marshall answered "yes" to the first two questions and "no" to the third. His reasoning was as follows.

1. Does Marbury have a right to the appointment?

Marshall reasoned that the appointment had been signed by the President and sealed by the Secretary of State; therefore, Marbury had the right to hold the office for five years as provided by law.

2. Do the laws of the country give Marbury a way to have things set right?

Marshall reasoned that the Secretary of State is an officer of the government directed by the Constitution and laws made by Congress to perform certain duties such as delivering the documents. When the Secretary of State refused to do so, he broke the law and violated Marbury's rights. Marbury had the right to go to a court and ask it to order the Secretary of State to deliver his document and to give him the job approved by the President.

3. Is asking the Supreme Court for a writ of mandamus the right way for Marbury to try to set things right?

On this point, Marshall said "no". He argued that the part of the Judiciary Act that gave Marbury the right to ask the Supreme Court to issue a writ of mandamus was unconstitutional. The Constitution clearly limits the Supreme Court's original jurisdiction, that is, the cases it can hear without their first being heard by a lower court, to "cases affecting ambassadors, other public ministers and consuls, and those in which a state shall be a party." Marbury was not an ambassador, a minister, consul, or a state, so the Supreme Court did not have the power to hear his case unless it was first heard in a lower court and then appealed to the Supreme Court.

Marshall reasoned that the part of the Judiciary Act that gave Marbury the right to have his case heard by the Supreme Court changed the Constitution. Since Congress did not have the authority to change the Constitution, that part of the Judiciary Act was unconstitutional.

Chief Justice Marshall did not order Secretary Madison to deliver the documents. Thus, the Court avoided the almost certain embarrassment of having the president, Thomas Jefferson, refuse to obey the Court's order. In the process, Marshall gained a much more important power for the Supreme Court. By declaring a part of the Judiciary Act unconstitutional, the Supreme Court gained the power of judicial review to declare acts of Congress and the President unconstitutional simply by exercising it.

The Supreme Court as the guardian of the people's Constitution

In the beginning of this lesson, you were asked to take a position on whether or not the Supreme Court should have the power of judicial review over acts of Congress. This is the question Chief Justice Marshall dealt with in the case of *Marbury v. Madison,* and he decided the Court should have this power.

Marshall justified his decision with the following argument. When the people of this nation adopted the Constitution to be the supreme law of the land, they had consented to be governed by its rules, which included important limitations upon the powers of Congress. When Congress violates those limitations, it has violated the will of the people. If the Supreme Court were not to have the power of judicial review, there would be no effective way to enforce the limitations the people have placed upon the powers of Congress in the Constitution. Its powers would be unlimited, and we would no longer have a constitutional government.

Reviewing and using the lesson

1. What is "judicial review"?

2. Outline the facts of the Supreme Court case by which judicial review became an accepted principle of our system of government. By what reasoning did Chief Justice John Marshall reach his decision?

3. One of the central principles of democratic government is that the will of the majority, expressed through its representatives, must prevail. The practice of judicial review may contradict this principle. How? What arguments can you develop in support of judicial review?

4. If you do not approve of the practice of judicial review, what alternative would you propose for settling disagreements over the meaning of the Constitution? Defend your choice.

5. Compare *Marbury v. Madison* and the Virginia and Kentucky Resolutions as methods of controlling the power of the federal government.

Why are there continuing controversies over the interpretation of the Constitution?

Photograph by Josh Mathes, collection of the Supreme Court of the United States

The Supreme Court

Purpose of Lesson 22

Today most Americans agree that judicial review is a necessary power of the Supreme Court. They do not always agree, however, on how the Court should use this power. The Supreme Court often hears cases about which there are strong feelings and great controversy. The decisions of the Court in these cases have important results that may affect the day-to-day lives of millions of citizens. Many of these cases involve disagreements about the proper role of our government and the meaning of the Constitution.

Since the Supreme Court has been given the power to make final decisions about the interpretation of the Constitution, it is inevitable that some people will support its decisions and some will criticize them. These disagreements are often over the methods used to interpret the Constitution. In this lesson you will learn about three different methods of interpreting the Constitution.

When you have completed the lesson, you should be able to summarize these methods and the arguments for and against each of them. Some phrases contained in the lesson which you should be able to explain are listed below.

literal meaning of the Constitution
intent of the Framers
basic principles and values
perspective of history

The problem of interpreting the Constitution

Once the Supreme Court agrees to hear a case on a constitutional issue, the justices face the difficult question of deciding whether or not the federal government or a state government has violated the Constitution. Understanding the meaning of some parts of the Constitution is fairly easy since some parts of it are quite specific and their meaning is clear. For example, there is little disagreement about what is meant when the Constitution says that:

- a person has to be 35 years old to be president, or

- no tax shall be placed on goods exported from a state.

However, as you have seen in previous lessons, not all parts of the Constitution are so clear. For example, what does it mean when the Constitution says the following?

- Congress shall have the power to make laws which it decides are "necessary and proper" to carry out its responsibilities.

- Citizens are protected against "unreasonable searches and seizures."

- No state shall "deprive any person of life, liberty, or property without due process of law."

The Framers knew that deciding on the meaning of such parts of the Constitution would be a continuing process throughout the history of the nation. The problem of how to interpret the Constitution has not been solved. Even justices of the Supreme Court disagree about the best method of interpretation. For this reason, among others, many important decisions of the Supreme Court have been made by a majority vote of five to four of the nine justices.

The controversies over how the Constitution should be interpreted often focus upon which of three different methods should be used to interpret the Constitution. These methods, and the arguments for and against them, follow.

1. Using the literal meaning of the words in the Constitution.

With this method of interpretation, the justices should consider the literal or plain meaning of the words in the Constitution, or study what the words meant at the time they were written, and base their decisions upon them.

Argument in support:

The Court's decisions should be based, as closely as possible, on how the Framers meant the Constitution to be interpreted. If the meaning of the <u>words</u> is clear, then this is the best way to find out what they meant. Also, by relying on the plain meaning, the law becomes certain and predictable.

Argument against:

It is difficult to know the exact meaning of many of the words and important phrases in the Constitution. There was even disagreement about their meaning at the time of the Convention and shortly after it. Consider, for example, the disagreements among Alexander Hamilton, James Madison, and Thomas Jefferson over the meaning of the "necessary and proper" clause. Besides, the Framers and other Founders did not intend later generations to be restricted to eighteenth-century interpretations, since moral, social, and political standards change.

2. Using the intentions of the men who wrote the Constitution.

The justices of the Supreme Court and of the lower courts should only make decisions based upon how the Framers would have made them. To find how the Framers would have made the decisions, the justices should read the records of the Philadelphia Convention, the state conventions that ratified the Constitution, and the congressional debates over the amendments.

Argument in Support:

This approach is the most faithful to the basic ideas contained in the Constitution. It limits the ability of justices to base their decisions on their own personal preferences. If the justices cannot find out what the Framers would have done with regard to an act of Congress or some other branch of government, they should not declare it unconstitutional.

Argument Against:

On many questions about the meaning of the Constitution, it is difficult, if not impossible, to discover exactly what was intended. First, this approach would require studying the ideas of the fifty-five men who attended the Philadelphia Convention and the ideas of the leaders of all of the state conventions that ratified the Constitution. Then it would require deciding which of the Framers' ideas should be counted. Even when the intentions of some men were clear, the intentions of others were not, and there were often disagreements about the meaning of particular parts of the Constitution. Second, the Founders had no ideas about such twentieth-century developments as airline travel or wire tapping. They intended each generation to give its own meaning to the Constitution. To rely on their intentions, which were formed two hundred years ago, might preserve outmoded ways of doing things and some practices which are no longer acceptable, such as slavery and racial segregation.

3. Using basic principles and values in the perspective of history.

The Constitution contains basic ideas, principles, and values about government and the role that it should play in our lives. These include the natural rights philosophy, the principles of constitutionalism, and the values of republican government as they were understood by the Founders. The justices should base their decisions on these basic ideas taking into account the nation's history and the changes in morality and social policy that have taken place.

Argument in Support:

Justices' decisions should be based upon their understanding of ideas such as freedom, justice, and equality, and what they mean today. The way we look at some of these ideas is very different from the way the Founders looked at them 200 years ago, and the decisions of the Supreme Court should take these differences into account. It is these general, larger goals that the Founders wanted to achieve, and the justices should do their best to adapt them to modern society.

Argument Against:

This approach gives the justices too much freedom to decide cases according to their own political and moral preferences. Since there are no clear and precise ways to decide how to apply such ideas as freedom, justice, and equality to specific situations, justices would be free to apply them as they wished. This could mean a justice's position about what is just or fair might be different from the position of a majority of members of Congress. This would violate the basic idea of representative democracy by allowing a few justices to overrule the action of the majority of the legislature, which was elected by the people.

Judicial review in practice

In practice, justices tend to be influenced by many considerations. These include their interpretations of the language of the Constitution and the intent of the Founders; the precedents justices have established in previous cases; current social policies and political and economic concerns; and their personal and political beliefs.

Yet, despite these influences, the justices are conscious of their responsibility to rule on the constitutionality of the issues involved, and not on the basis of their own personal feelings. This may mean that the Supreme Court will rule that a law is constitutional even if the justices feel that it is unwise. As Chief Justice Warren Burger stated, when reviewing an act of Congress:

> Its wisdom is not the concern of the courts; if a challenged action does not violate the Constitution, it must be sustained . . . . By the same token, the fact that a given law or procedure is efficient, convenient, and useful in facilitating functions of government, standing alone, will not save it if it is contrary to the Constitution. *(INS v. Chadha, 1983)*

While it would be unrealistic to pretend that the personal preferences of justices never affect the decisions of the Court, it is reasonable to claim that the continued authority of the Court depends on its being faithful to both the language and spirit of the Constitution.

The Supreme Court's decisions have been particularly controversial when they have attempted to define and protect certain basic rights. The next lessons will deal with some of the decisions the Court has made regarding equal protection of the laws, due process of law, freedom of religion, and freedom of expression.

Reviewing and using the lesson

1. In the light of what you have learned about judicial review, which of the following positions of the Founders would you agree with? Explain the bases of your answers.

> It is. . . of great importance. . . to examine. . . the judicial power, because those who are to be vested with it, are to be placed in a situation altogether unprecedented in a free country. . . They are independent of the people, of the legislature, and of every power under heaven. Men placed in this situation will generally soon feel themselves independent of heaven itself...If the legislature pass any laws, inconsistent with the sense the judges put upon the constitution, they will declare it void; and therefore in this respect their power is superior to that of the legislature... (*Letters of Brutus*, 1787)

> . . . the judiciary, from the nature of its functions, will always be the least dangerous... It may truly be said to have neither Force nor Will, but merely judgement. . . A constitution is, in fact, and must be regarded by the judges, as a fundamental law. It therefore belongs to them to ascertain its meaning. . . (Alexander Hamilton, *The Federalist*, No. 78, 1788)

> . . . the opinion which gives to the judges the right to decide what laws are constitutional, and what not. . . would make the Judiciary a despotic branch. (Thomas Jefferson)

2. Which of the following statements by former justices of the Supreme Court do you agree with? Explain your position.

> [The Constitution] is intended to endure for ages to come, and consequently, to be adapted to the various crises of human affairs. (Chief Justice Marshall)

> We are under a Constitution, but the Constitution is what the judges say it is. (Charles Evans Hughes, Chief Justice of the United States)

> As a member of this court I am not justified in writing my opinions into the Constitution, no matter how deeply I may cherish them. (Justice Felix Frankfurter)

> The case before us must be considered in the light of our whole experience and not merely in that of what was said a hundred years ago. (Justice Oliver Wendell Holmes)

How has power been delegated to the federal and state governments?

Purpose of Lesson 23

The purpose of this lesson is to increase your understanding of the federal system created under the Constitution. It also discusses one of the first important Supreme Court opinions that deals with the division of power between the federal and state governments. Finally, it will introduce you to some of the continuing problems of the relationship between the nation and the states.

When you complete the lesson, you should be able to describe the basic characteristics of a federal system and give a brief explanation of the Court's opinion and its importance. Basic ideas and terms included in this lesson are as follows.

sovereignty
federal system
McCulloch v. Maryland
unitary government
confederation

How is the system of government created by the Framers different from others?

Our system of government, created by the Framers, is quite complicated. It differed in two important ways from other systems of government that existed at the time the Constitution was written. These are explained below.

1. <u>Sovereignty,</u> or ultimate authority, is in the people. In other nations, the ultimate authority was thought to be held by the government even if it had received that authority from the people. For example, in some nations the king was sovereign. In Great Britain, the Parliament was sovereign.

In the Preamble to the Constitution, the Framers set forth this new idea of sovereignty when they wrote, "We the People of the United States . . . do ordain and establish this Constitution for the United States of America." Under this new system, sovereignty remains in "the people," who give certain powers to the government. The government has these delegated powers, but the people remain the supreme authority.

2. Our government is a <u>federal system</u>. This means that the people have not delegated all of the powers of government to one central government. Instead, the people of the various states have delegated certain powers to their state governments in their state constitutions. As citizens of the nation, they have delegated certain powers to the federal government in the United States Constitution. And finally, certain powers have been kept by the people and not delegated to any government. This complicated form of organization is called a federal system.

Other kinds of governments

Before our government was established under the Constitution, most nations had been organized in one of two ways. These were <u>unitary governments</u> and <u>confederate governments,</u> or <u>confederations.</u>

Unitary governments were those in which a central government acted directly upon the citizens. Great Britain had a unitary government during this period and still has.

In contrast, a confederation, or a "federal union," as it was sometimes called, is a government whose parts are states rather than individuals. This meant that states that were members of a confederation kept full control over anything that affected their own citizens and territory. States would unite in a confederation for certain purposes such as defense and the regulation of trade.

The government of the confederation would act upon the member states, not upon the citizens of those states. The government under the Articles of Confederation was a confederation. The United Nations is a modern example of a confederation.

The Constitution established a system that is a combination of both unitary and confederate systems.

- It is like a confederate government because it was ratified by state conventions, amendments are ratified by states, senators were originally chosen by state legislatures, and each state is represented by the same number of senators. In addition the power of the central government is limited to certain responsibilities.

- It is like a unitary government because the members of the House of Representatives are elected by the people from electoral districts of equal population. Most important, it acts directly upon the people in fulfilling the responsibilities it has been given by the Constitution.

The result of this complicated system is that both the federal and the state governments have certain powers over individual citizens while sovereignty remains with the citizens. This system has many possibilities for disputes, most of which come down to the simple question, "Which powers have been delegated to which government?" This question was raised during the ratification debates and has remained one of the central issues in American politics ever since.

The supremacy of the federal government

There were many disagreements at the Philadelphia Convention over what powers the federal government should have. However, there was no doubt that whatever those powers were, they were superior to those of the state governments. This is the meaning of Article VI which reads, "This constitution and the laws of the United States . . . shall be the <u>supreme law of the Land</u> . . . . "

Federalism and the supremacy clause

As we have learned, the people are the ultimate source of the power of the federal and state governments in the United States. They have delegated this power to these governments to protect their rights and to promote the common welfare. We have also learned that the supremacy clause clearly indicates that federal laws are to be considered superior to any state laws with which they may conflict.

Conflict between federal and state power

A dispute about the power of the federal government over the states occurred in 1819 in the case of *McCulloch v. Maryland.* As in an earlier dispute you have studied, it involved a bank created by the federal government, the Second Bank of the United States. The Bank was extremely unpopular in the southern and western states. People there argued that the Bank favored the interests of wealthy shippers and merchants, and that it gave the federal government too much power. Attempts were made to prevent its operation. In 1818, the Maryland legislature placed a heavy tax on all banks not chartered by the state. McCulloch, the cashier at the Baltimore branch of the Bank of the United States, refused to pay the tax and was sued by the state of Maryland. The state courts upheld the right of Maryland to tax the federal bank. McCulloch appealed to the Supreme Court.

McCulloch v. Maryland was one of the most important cases to be decided in the early days of the Supreme Court. Two key issues were involved. First, did Congress have the power to create a bank? Second, could the state of Maryland tax a branch of the federal bank?

The Supreme Court ruled that Congress did have the authority to create the bank. Chief Justice John Marshall said that this power was given to the Congress by the "necessary and proper" clause of the Constitution that we discussed in an earlier lesson. He upheld the reasoning Hamilton had used earlier to persuade President Washington to sign the legislation creating the First Bank of the United States.

Turning to the second issue, Marshall insisted that the authority of the federal government comes from the people rather than from the state governments. The Constitution had not been adopted by state governments, but by the people gathered in state conventions. Therefore, the Constitution gained its authority from the people. For this reason, the federal government, in fulfilling the responsibilities given it by the Constitution and ultimately by the people, is superior to the state governments. This is

why the Framers included the supremacy clause, he argued.

Basing his argument on the supremacy clause, Marshall held that when a state law conflicts with a federal law, the federal law must be obeyed. Maryland's attempt to tax the federal bank was, therefore, illegal, for "the power to tax involves the power to destroy." Marshall argued that if federal agencies could be taxed by the states, their existence would be dependent on the will of the states. The American people, Marshall claimed, did not design their federal government to make it dependent on the states.

Marshall's ruling in *McCulloch v. Maryland* clearly established the supremacy of the federal government within its sphere of authority and greatly increased the powers of Congress.

The power of the federal government today

Citizens make greater demands upon the federal government today than they did in the past. In addition, the United States' political and military role in the world has greatly increased. As a result, the federal government now has far more power than anything the Framers could have imagined.

Since 1937, the Supreme Court has interpreted the Constitution to give increased power to the federal government. In some ways it can be argued that what the Anti-Federalists feared has indeed happened: the federal government now has power over many areas of people's lives that used to be controlled only by the states or by the people themselves.

There are two important points to remember about the question of federalism today:

1. Most of the decisions about how much power is to be left to the states are made by Congress, not by the Supreme Court on constitutional grounds. This is because the Supreme Court has interpreted the Constitution to give the federal government more power than it had in the past. Congress decides, on the basis of practical considerations, whether the federal or state governments should fulfill certain responsibilities the citizens think should be fulfilled.

2. In spite of the increased power of the federal government, most of the laws that affect us directly are state laws, including most property law, contract law, family law, and criminal law.

The power of the federal government is not limited, of course, to making laws. Indeed, it is increasingly common for the federal government to attempt to influence state law by the use of federal funds. For example, the federal government has used highway funds to encourage the states to set the speed limit at 55 miles an hour. If a state does not agree to do this, it does not receive the federal funds.

The Framers could not possibly have predicted what the relation between the power of the states and the power of the federal government would be 200 years later. The complexities of the new system of political organization they created, as well as the realities governments confront, make it equally unlikely that we can predict with a high degree of accuracy the nature of the relationship in the future.

Reviewing and using the lesson

1. Define "sovereignty."

2. Where does sovereignty for the United States government lie? What evidence can you give as support for your answer?

3. Explain what a federal system is.

4. *McCulloch v. Maryland* is considered one of the most important Supreme Court decisions in our history. Discuss its stand on (a) the "necessary and proper" clause and (b) the supremacy clause.

5. In *McCulloch v. Maryland* what position did the Court take on the question of federal authority versus states' rights? What reasons did the Court give for its opinion?

6. List examples of situations in which the federal government attempts to influence state laws by using federal funds.

7. It has been said that the history of our nation is the history of the expanding power of the federal government. What is your opinion about this expansion of federal power? Is it good or bad for the nation? Explain your position.

Unit Five: Fundamental Rights

Women vote in a Boston municipal election in 1888, 32 years before the 19th Amendment

Purpose of Unit Five

You have learned in the earlier units that one of the most important purposes of our government is the protection of the basic rights of the people. You should also be aware that during the early years of this nation, many of the rights set forth in the Declaration of Independence and the Constitution were actually enjoyed by relatively few people. Over the last two hundred years, great progress has been made in closing the gap between the ideals expressed in those documents and the reality of the daily life of the people of our nation. The lessons in this unit will briefly describe the importance of the basic rights guaranteed to the people in the Constitution and how they have been extended to many of those deprived of them in the past.

How does the Constitution promote equal protection of the laws?

Purpose of Lesson 24

The Fourteenth Amendment to the Constitution was ratified in 1868, just after the Civil War. The <u>equal protection clause</u> of this amendment has become the most important protection in the Constitution used to prevent unfair discrimination against people by the state governments. The history of the attempt to use this clause is filled with conflict. Its application by the courts in recent years has resulted in abolishing a great deal of discrimination in our society and in the taking of positive steps to remedy the effects of past discrimination.

When you complete this lesson, you should be able to explain the equal protection clause and some of the changes that have been made in its interpretation since its inclusion in the Constitution. Basic ideas and terms introduced which you should be able to explain are listed below.

> **Civil War Amendments**
> **Fourteenth Amendment**
> **equal protection of the laws**
> **"Jim Crow" laws**
> **"separate but equal"**
> **segregation**
> <u>**Plessy v. Ferguson**</u>
> <u>**Brown v. Board of Education**</u>

Problem solving

Examining examples of discrimination

Before studying the history of the equal protection clause in this lesson, review the following examples of discrimination. Each illustrates an issue involving the equal protection clause that has been dealt with by the federal courts. Explain which of these examples of discrimination by a local or state government you think should be considered unconstitutional.

1. Your state has a law that says that you and all students of your race must go to separate schools from the other students in your community.

2. Your city has an ordinance saying that you and your family cannot live in certain sections of town because of your religious beliefs.

3. Your state has a law saying that you can only marry someone of the same race.

4. Your city fire department will not hire you because you are a woman.

5. You and a friend of the opposite sex work for the state and do the same type and amount of work. Yet you discover that you are paid considerably less than your friend.

The Civil War Amendments

The history of the Fourteenth Amendment, which limits the powers of state governments, begins shortly after the Civil War ended slavery in America. At that time, three amendments, commonly called the Civil War Amendments, were added to the Constitution:

- The Thirteenth Amendment abolished slavery in the United States.

- The Fourteenth Amendment granted the newly freed slaves national and state citizenship.

- The Fifteenth Amendment guaranteed to the new citizens the right to vote.

But the Fourteenth Amendment, which is addressed to the states, contains two additional clauses that many scholars consider among the most important in the entire Constitution: a <u>due process</u> clause and the <u>equal protection</u> clause. These clauses have been the basis for some of the most important interpretations of the Constitution the Supreme Court has made--interpretations which have affected the lives of all of us. In Lessons 26 and 27 you will learn of the importance of the due process clause. In this lesson you will learn of the history and importance of the equal protection clause and a few of the areas of life to which it has been applied.

The equal protection clause

The equal protection clause of the Fourteenth Amendment says: "No State shall . . . deny to any person within its jurisdiction the equal protection of the laws." At the time of its ratification, in 1868, this clause, like the rest of the Fourteenth Amendment, was intended to prevent discrimination against blacks and to guarantee them the rights that go along with equal citizenship. But, as we shall see, it did not begin to serve this purpose until almost one hundred years later.

It should be noted that, after the Civil War, when Congress was considering the amendments to free the slaves, grant them citizenship, and guarantee them the right to vote, women leaders of the anti-slavery movement, including Susan B. Anthony, asked that the right to vote for women be included in the amendments. The male anti-slavery leaders refused to do so. Instead, they specifically included the term "male citizen" for the first time in the Constitution, in the second section of the Fourteenth Amendment. The later successful fight for women's right to vote will be discussed in Lesson 25.

Changing interpretations of the meaning of "equal protection of the laws"

In the years following the passage of the Fourteenth Amendment, blacks found it difficult to gain the equal rights guaranteed to them by the Constitution. A number of state governments passed "Jim Crow" laws requiring blacks to use separate schools and other public facilities. The states claimed that such laws did not violate the equal protection clause because the separate facilities were equal. The Supreme Court considered this argument in two famous cases.

Plessy v. Ferguson (1896)

Suppose your state passed laws saying that because of your race, you could not use the same public bathrooms, water fountains, seats on buses or trains, or other public facilities that other citizens could use. However, separate facilities which were supposed to be equal to those used by others were set aside for your use. Would you say that your state was providing you with the "equal protection of the laws"?

The case of *Plessy v. Ferguson* involved this "separate but equal" argument, that is, that a state government was treating blacks equally when it re-

quired them to use segregated facilities if the facilities provided were equal.

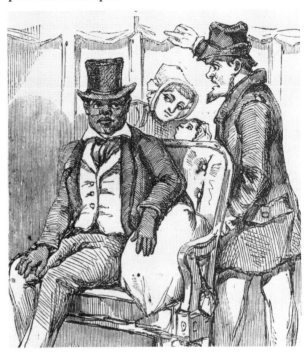

Library of Congress

Cartoon from Illustrated London News, 1856

The State of Louisiana had passed a law requiring railroad companies to provide "equal but separate" cars for white and black passengers. A committee was formed by black leaders to test the constitutionality of the law. They chose Homer Plessy to make their test case. He bought a ticket but he insisted on riding in the cars for whites and refused to ride in the cars for blacks. Plessy was arrested and convicted in the state courts, and eventually his case was appealed to the Supreme Court. The Court was asked to decide whether the law requiring "separate but equal" treatment of blacks was unfair discrimination by the state government in violation of the equal protection of the laws clause of the Fourteenth Amendment.

The Supreme Court held that the Constitution had not been violated. The Court said that to separate the races did not in itself suggest one race was inferior to the other. Since the law required that blacks and whites be provided equal facilities, the Court concluded there was no discrimination and, therefore, the law was constitutional.

Justice John Marshall Harlan disagreed and wrote a strong dissenting opinion. He argued that the segregation law, passed by whites who dominated the state government in Louisiana, definitely was unfair to

91

blacks and implied that they were inferior. Therefore, it was clearly in violation of the Constitution. He said the promise of "equal" facilities was a false promise made to avoid providing blacks the equal protection of the laws which they were guaranteed by the Constitution.

The "separate but equal" argument contained in *Plessy v. Ferguson* was the Supreme Court's position on racial segregation for almost sixty years. Federal and state legislatures continued to tolerate, and in some cases, encourage discrimination against minorities. Until the 1930s, the Court's interpretations of the Fourteenth Amendment gave little responsibility or power to the federal government to protect citizens from racial discrimination by state governments or by private citizens. Since 1954, however, there have been significant changes in the way the Supreme Court has viewed the equal protection clause of the Fourteenth Amendment. The landmark in this shift came in the case of *Brown v. Board of Education.*

Brown v. Board of Education (1954)

Suppose your state passed a law saying that you were not allowed to go to certain public schools because of the color of your skin. Instead, you and all students like you were forced to attend special schools for your group which were supposedly equal in physical facilities and quality of teaching to the schools attended by other students, but separated from them. Would you say that your state was providing you with the "equal protection of the laws"?

Linda Brown lived five blocks from a neighborhood elementary school, but because of her race, she was forced to attend the school for black children twenty-one blocks away. Her parents sued the school board of Topeka, Kansas, for denying their seven-year-old daughter admission to a neighborhood school set aside "for whites only." The Browns were represented by an attorney for the National Association for the Advancement of Colored People, Thurgood Marshall, who later became the first black justice of the Supreme Court. Marshall argued that the practice of having segregated public schools violated the equal protection clause because it placed black children at a severe disadvantage.

In hearing the argument in this case, the Supreme Court asked the attorneys to address themselves to two questions:

- What historical evidence was there that the authors of the 14th Amendment <u>intended</u> it to prohibit segregation in public schools?

Justice Thurgood Marshall

- If the intention of its authors is not clear, was it within the power of the Court to abolish public school segregation if the Court concluded that the state was violating the equal protection clause of the Fourteenth Amendment?

As you can see, the justices used the ideas about how to interpret the Constitution we discussed in Lesson 22 in making their decision in this issue of racial segregation. In deciding to overrule *Plessy v. Ferguson,* they agreed to reject the "separate but equal" theory which had stood for over fifty years.

The Supreme Court decided that whether the authors of the Fourteenth Amendment intended it to prevent racial discrimination in public schools could not be determined. They also decided that it was within the power of the Court to abolish discrimination on the basis of the principles of the equal protection clause.

On May 17, 1954, Chief Justice Earl Warren delivered the unanimous decision of the Supreme Court.

> To separate [children] from others of similar age and qualifications solely because of their race generates a feeling of inferiority as to their status in the community that may affect their hearts and minds in a way unlikely ever to be undone . . . . Whatever may have been

the extent of psychological knowledge at the time of *Plessy v. Ferguson*, this finding is amply supported by modern authority . . . . Any language in *Plessy v. Ferguson* contrary to this finding is rejected . . . . Separate educational facilities are inherently unequal . . . . [We] hold that the plaintiffs . . . [are] deprived of the equal protection of the laws guaranteed by the Fourteenth Amendment.

The President orders federal troops to enforce the law

Most southern states resisted the Court's order to integrate their schools "with all deliberate speed." In so doing, they raised the issue of how far the federal government can, or should, go to be sure that the decisions of the Supreme Court are carried out. In one case, when the Governor of Arkansas refused to obey a court order and tried to stop black students from entering a previously all white public high school in Little Rock, President Dwight Eisenhower ordered the United States Army to go to that city to prevent the state from continuing its segregation policies.

Library of Congress

U..S. Soldiers in front of Central High School, Little Rock, Arkansas, 1957

The national movement to end unfair discrimination

At the same time that the Supreme Court was trying to end racial discrimination in the public schools, Congress, the executive branch, and many groups in the general public were also working to end racial discrimination. As early as 1947, the report of President Harry S. Truman's Committee on Civil Rights called for an end to racial discrimination in education, housing, employment, voting, and all other areas of American life. Over the next twenty years, great efforts were made to end racial discrimination and guarantee all citizens equality of opportunity. The 1954 decision in the *Brown* case, important as it was, dealt only with the issue of racial segregation in the schools. It did not protect blacks from other forms of public and private discrimination. In the 1960s, sit-ins, freedom rides, and mass demonstrations by blacks and some whites played a key role in mobilizing public opinion in support of the elimination of other forms of discrimination against blacks.

In response to the pressures for social change of the 1960s, and the policies of presidents John F. Kennedy and Lyndon B. Johnson, the Civil Rights Acts of 1964, 1965, and 1968 were passed. Their purpose was to implement the ideals of the 13th, 14th, and 15th Amendments--almost a hundred years after their passage. In addition, Congress passed the Voting Rights Act of 1965 which protected the voting rights of blacks. A few years later, Congress passed the Fair Housing Act, which prohibited discrimination in the rental, sale, and advertising of housing.

In response to public pressure, Congress has taken steps to prevent other forms of discrimination. The Equal Employment Opportunities Act passed by Congress in 1968 has been used to prevent discrimination in job opportunities on the basis of sex or age. And Title IX (Education Act, 1972) bans discrimination on the basis of sex in any educational program that receives federal aid.

Continuing disagreements over "equal protection of the laws"

The attempt to eliminate discrimination and provide equal opportunities to all citizens is a continuing and controversial process. In this lesson, we have focused upon the use of the equal protection clause to protect the educational opportunities of blacks. However, the protections of the Fourteenth Amendment are not limited to blacks, but apply to all people who may face discrimination.

Today, disagreements continue about how much power, as well as responsibility, the federal government should have to prevent discrimination. Some of the important issues today involve claims by a variety of groups that they are still the victims of both public and private discrimination.

The issue of discrimination is a difficult one. Sometimes there are good and fair reasons for treating certain groups of people differently. For example, few people would argue that a law that says that people under the age of 16 may not be licensed to drive is unreasonable and unfair, even though there may be some individual 15-year-olds--or even 14-year-olds--who are capable of driving skillfully and safely. The state has the responsibility to protect its citizens, and the courts hesitate to declare laws unconstitutional if the laws are reasonable ways to do this.

However, when a law treats a person or group of people differently from others without good reason, it may be found to be a violation of the equal protection of the laws and thus unconstitutional. Laws that deprive people of rights just because of their race, sex, age, or ethnic background violate the principle that we have certain rights regardless of any of these factors.

Reviewing and using the lesson

1. What restrictions does the Fourteenth Amendment place on the state governments? Why has this clause become such an important part of the entire Constitution? Give an example of this clause as it has been, or may be, used which would demonstrate its importance.

2. What position regarding racial segregation did the Supreme Court take in the case of *Plessy v. Ferguson*? What was its reasoning?

3. Compare the *Plessy* decision with the decision in *Brown v. Board of Education* of 1954. Select a portion of the Court's opinion in the *Brown* case which directly contradicts the *Plessy* opinion.

4. Treating categories of people differently may be reasonable or unreasonable. Give an example of such treatment which you consider reasonable. If a state government passes a law treating some of its citizens differently for what it considers a good reason, and other citizens regard the law as unfair, how may the disagreement be resolved?

5. What conflicts might arise among the following important rights contained in the Constitution?

- the right to equal protection of the laws

- the right to privacy

- the right to property

- the right to freedom of association

For example, is it fair to have a private club which only allows men as members? Why or why not?

94

How has the right to vote expanded since the adoption of the Constitution?

Library of Congress

Women urge Congress that they be granted the right to vote on the basis of the 14th and 15th Amendments

Purpose of Lesson 25

Suffrage, that is, the right to vote, has been a subject of controversy throughout our history. During the colonial period and the early years of our nation, voting was generally restricted to white men who owned property. While the majority of white males qualified for suffrage, other people such as women, blacks, American Indians, and members of certain religious groups were usually denied the right to vote. In this lesson, we will look at how the right to vote has been extended over the last two hundred years to almost every citizen over eighteen years of age--the extension of representative democracy.

When you have completed this lesson, you should be able to describe the extension of voting rights as a result of changes in the voting laws in the various states, amendments to the Constitution, and decisions of the Supreme Court. You should also be able to describe how the extension of the right to vote is related to some of the fundamental ideas and principles about constitutional government that you have studied. Basic terms and ideas in this lesson which you should be able to explain are listed below.

    suffrage
    Fifteenth Amendment
    poll taxes
    literacy tests
    grandfather clauses
    Twenty-Fourth Amendment
    Nineteenth Amendment
    Twenty-Sixth Amendment

The Constitution and the right to vote

At the Philadelphia Convention, the Framers could not agree on who should have the right to vote. As a result, the Constitution simply stated that members of the House of Representatives were to be elected by the people in each state who, under state law, were eligible to vote for the lower house of their state legislature.

The Constitution, therefore, left to each state government the power to decide who could vote. As a result, many of the early battles over suffrage took place at the state level. Some of the most important steps in this struggle to end discrimination in suffrage are described below.

From the Founding to the Civil War
Extending the right to vote to all white males

You require that a man shall have sixty dollars worth of property, or he shall not vote. Very well, take an illustration. Here is a man who today owns a jackass, and the jackass is worth sixty dollars. Today the man is a voter and he goes to the polls and deposits his vote. Tomorrow the jackass dies. The next day the man comes to vote without his jackass and he cannot vote at all. Now tell me, which was the voter, the man or the jackass? (Story of Thomas Paine, 1737-1809)

As you have learned, white men had the right to vote and take part in government, but usually they had to meet certain qualifications. However, the period before the Civil War was marked by an increase in the number of white men who did gain the right to vote. For example:

- During the Revolutionary War, six state governments eliminated all property requirements and gave the right to vote to all white males, rich or poor. But at the same time, three other state governments increased the property requirements, limiting the right to vote. In some states, the right to vote included the requirement that a person belong to a particular religious group.

- Following the election of Thomas Jefferson as president in 1800, many states began to eliminate the property requirement for voting. Between 1812 and 1821, six new western states became part of the nation and these gave the vote to all white males. During the same period, four of the older states that had property requirements abolished them.

- Andrew Jackson ran for President in 1828. His support came from many men who had just won the right to vote. During this period, suffrage continued to be extended to more white males.

- By the 1840s, almost every state government had given all white males the right to vote. Only two states still had any significant property qualifications. Restrictions on voting by Catholics and non-Christians were eliminated. In a few states, even immigrants not yet naturalized were given the right to vote. The last state to change, North Carolina, abandoned its property test in 1856.

It should not be assumed that the gains that were made during this period were easily achieved or that feelings did not run high. The situation in Rhode Island, where over half the white males were denied the right to vote, led to Dorr's Rebellion of 1842. This unsuccessful struggle is an example of the difficulty of expanding the right to vote during the first part of the 1800s. Despite the gains, it should not be forgotten that the right to vote was still restricted to white males, and only those over twenty-one years of age.

Library of Congress
Black men vote for the first time after the Civil War

96

From the Civil War to present times
Extending the right to vote to black males

The Fifteenth Amendment was added to the Constitution in 1870, just after the Civil War. It says:

Section 1. The right of citizens of the United States to vote shall not be denied or abridged by the United States or by any State on account of race, color, or previous condition of servitude.

Section 2. The Congress shall have the power to enforce this article by appropriate legislation.

The intent of this amendment was to give black males the right to vote. Unfortunately, just changing the Constitution or passing a law does not necessarily mean that what you wish to happen will happen. During the early part of this period, the Supreme Court left to the state governments the responsibility for protecting most of the basic rights of their citizens. There were many people in the southern states who did not want black males to have the right to vote or to have a role in the government. Although the Fifteenth Amendment guaranteed the right to vote to black males, the state governments passed laws that made it almost impossible for them to exercise their newly-won right. Some of the ways they did this are described below.

- Poll taxes. Some state governments passed laws that required citizens to pay a tax before they could vote. These were called "poll taxes." Since most former slaves were very poor, they were unable to pay the tax. In a number of the states, poor white men were allowed to vote even when they could not pay the poll tax.

- Literacy tests. Some of the state governments also passed laws requiring men to take tests to prove that they could read and write before they were allowed to vote. These were called "literacy tests" and were very difficult for blacks, who had not had an opportunity to get an adequate education, to pass. But literacy tests also eliminated educated blacks because they were administered unfairly so that blacks would fail and whites, even though illiterate, would pass.

- Grandfather clauses. Another method used to stop black men from voting was the use of laws that contained "grandfather clauses." These clauses limited the right to vote to people who were descendants of those who had previously had the right to vote. This obviously did not include former slaves.

Other methods used to deprive black citizens of their rights were those that were not employed directly by state governments but by private individuals and organizations who were usually not prosecuted by state authorities for their illegal activities against blacks. Among these were torture and murder, carried out by groups like the Ku Klux Klan, to terrorize black citizens so that they would not try to exercise their constitutional rights.

Some of the restrictive voting laws that were enacted by state governments were not declared unconstitutional by the Supreme Court until 1915, over forty-five years after the Fifteenth Amendment had been passed. Many of the laws that limited the right of blacks to vote lasted even longer than that.

As a result of the civil rights movement of the 1950s and 1960s, the federal government began using its power to protect the rights of blacks in the South against political discrimination. In 1964, the Twenty-Fourth Amendment was added to the Constitution prohibiting the use of poll taxes as a means of denying the right to vote in federal elections. The following year, Congress passed the Voting Rights Act which gave additional protection for voting rights by authorizing the federal government to take over registration of voters in areas where state officials had regularly prevented blacks from registering to vote. In 1966, the Supreme Court ruled that the use of poll taxes in state elections was a violation of the equal protection clause of the Fourteenth Amendment (*Harper v. Virginia Board of Elections*). Thus, by the mid-60s, great progress had been made in ensuring that blacks could enjoy the right to vote which had been guaranteed in the Fifteenth Amendment almost a century earlier.

Closely linked with the struggle of blacks for both freedom and equality was the struggle for women's rights. It took even longer for women to win the legal right to vote than it did for blacks.

Extending the right to vote to women

For most of the history of the United States, women did not have the right to vote or take part in government. Women were the largest group of people ever denied the right to vote in our country. The struggle for this right was long and difficult. It involved a challenge to strongly-held traditional beliefs about what the role of women should be in society. The following events illustrate this struggle.

- The Fourteenth Amendment includes the following: "All persons born or naturalized in the United States, and subject to the jurisdiction thereof, are citizens of the United States and of the State wherein they reside." In 1874, people in favor of women's rights argued in the Supreme Court that this clause gave women the right to vote. The Supreme Court denied their claim saying that being a citizen does not automatically give a person the right to vote, and that it was not unconstitutional for states to deny the vote to women.

National Portrait Gallery, Smithsonian Institution

Susan B. Anthony, 1820 - 1906

- In 1876, Susan B. Anthony led a delegation of women to the Philadelphia Centennial Celebration of the Declaration of Independence. Although no women had been invited to participate in the program, Anthony's protest included reading the Women's Declaration of Rights: "Yet we cannot forget, even in this glad hour, that while all men of every race . . . have been invested with the full rights of citizenship under our hospitable flag, all women still suffer the degradation of disfranchisement."

- Wyoming gave women the right to vote while it was still a territory. The story is told that when certain members of Congress argued against this "petticoat provision," the Wyoming legislature said it would prefer to stay out of the Union one hundred years rather than join it without allowing women to vote. Wyoming was allowed into the Union.

- After Wyoming, other western states quickly extended the right of suffrage to women. By the end of World War I, over half of the states had given women the right to vote.

- Pressure for a women's suffrage amendment mounted during World War I as women entered the work force in record numbers. In 1918, President Woodrow Wilson announced his support for the proposed amendment.

The uncertainty and slowness of state-by-state victories encouraged women to push harder for a constitutional amendment which would give them the right to vote. In 1920, even though there was still considerable opposition to granting women this right, the Nineteenth Amendment was finally ratified. Women had the right to vote after being denied that right for over 130 years. The Nineteenth Amendment says:

- The right of citizens of the United States to vote shall not be denied or abridged by the United States or by any State on account of sex.

- Congress shall have the power to enforce this article by appropriate legislation.

Extending the right to vote to eighteen-year-olds

Before 1971, only Alaska, Georgia, Hawaii, and Kentucky had allowed persons younger than twenty-one to participate in elections.

In 1970, Congress, in amending the Voting Rights Act, included a section which said no one should be denied the right to vote on the grounds of age who was eighteen years old or older. This law was challenged in the case of *Oregon v. Mitchell,* and the Supreme Court justices were divided in their opinions. Four justices decided that Congress had the power to lower the voting age to eighteen; four other justices concluded that Congress had no such power. Justice Hugo Black cast the decisive vote. He ruled that Congress could regulate the voting age in national elections but not in state elections. He argued that the Constitution leaves to the states the power to regulate the elections of their own public officials. The Congress does have the authority, however, to lower the voting age in federal elections.

Within six months of the Court decision, the Twenty-Sixth Amendment was ratified by the required number of states. It lowered the voting age to eighteen:

Section 1. The right of citizens of the United States, who are eighteen years of age or older, to vote shall not be denied or abridged by the United States or by any State on account of age.

Section 2. The Congress shall have the power to enforce this article by appropriate legislation.

Voter requirements today

Today almost every citizen of the United States eighteen years of age or older has the right to vote and take part in government. States can, however, pass some laws restricting the right to vote. The following outlines the present situation.

- Citizenship. The Constitution does not mention citizenship as a requirement for voting. In the past, as you know, some states allowed non-citizens to vote. Today, however, all states make citizenship a requirement of voting.

- Residence. All states have some kind of a residency requirement for voting. This means persons must live in the state and locality for a period of time before they can vote. The time that is required is not a long one, however-- usually only thirty days--because the Supreme Court has held longer periods to be unconstitutional.

- Age. No state can prevent anyone over eighteen years of age from voting on the basis of his or her age. Although none has done so, states can permit younger citizens to vote.

- Registration. Every state except North Dakota requires citizens to register with election officials and provide such information as name, age, and address in order to vote. The trend over the years has been to make this process easier and less time-consuming.

- Other qualifications. States also have a number of laws which can disqualify voters. For example, persons who are judged to be mentally incompetent, have been convicted of serious crimes or election fraud, or have been dishonorably discharged from the armed forces may be denied the right to vote.

Since almost all citizens now have the right to vote, the question of the suffrage is no longer as important or as controversial as it once was. Those who are concerned about the fate of representative democracy have turned their attention to other questions. Why do so many people who have the right to vote fail to exercise that right? How can the citizen acquire sufficient information to vote intelligently when government has become so complex? These are only two of the questions. What do you think are some of the other problems of representative democracy?

Reviewing and using the lesson

1. What did the Constitution of 1787 say about who had the right to vote?

2. Before the Civil War the right to vote was generally limited to white males. What restrictions were there on this right?

3. Before the Civil War, some limits on suffrage were gradually eliminated by the state governments. Since then, suffrage has been expanded by action of the federal government. Give specific examples of federal actions that have expanded the right to vote.

4. Except where forbidden by the federal government and the Constitution, the states today determine who may and who may not vote. What requirements do states place on the right to vote? Do you think they are reasonable? If not, why not?

5. Since the right to vote was given to all citizens eighteen years old and older, many people have been disappointed because so few people between the ages of eighteen and twenty-four exercise this right. Why do you suppose so few young people vote? Should they vote? Why?

What is due process of law?

Library of Congress

Children working in the cotton fields, 1912

Purpose of Lesson 26

In a previous lesson, attention was paid to the equal protection clause of the Fourteenth Amendment. In this lesson we will begin to look at another part of the Fourteenth Amendment, the <u>due process clause</u>. This clause is considered one of the most important in the Constitution. It has been the basis for many of the Supreme Court's decisions limiting the authority of both federal and state governments in order to protect the basic rights of the people.

You will learn the difference between <u>substantive</u> and <u>procedural due process</u> and how each protects your rights to life, liberty, and property. You will also learn about the process called incorporation which makes the most fundamental protections of the Bill of Rights apply against state actions.

When you have completed the lesson, you should be able to describe substantive due process and explain some of the changes in the application of this idea that have taken place. You should also be able to show how the protections of the Bill of Rights have been incorporated into the Fourteenth Amendment. Basic ideas and terms introduced in this lesson which you should be able to explain are listed below.

> **incorporation**
> **due process**
> **substantive due process**
> **procedural due process**
> **laissez faire**

Due Process and the Fourteenth Amendment

The due process clause of the Fourteenth Amendment says:

> nor shall any State deprive any person of life, liberty, or property, without due process of law . . . .

A due process clause also appears in the Fifth Amendment. But the Fifth Amendment and the rest of the Bill of Rights, as you have seen, originally applied only to the federal government. For more than the first hundred years of the history of our nation, the Bill of Rights was not applied to the acts of state governments. Gradually, after the Fourteenth Amendment was passed, this changed, and today most of our protections under the Bill of Rights are also protections against actions by state governments, through interpretations of the due process clause of that amendment.

What is due process of law?

It is impossible to give an exact definition of the phrase "due process of law." The term was first used in England in 1354, in a rewording of the Magna Carta. Its first use in an American constitution was in the Fifth Amendment, as part of the wording recommended by James Madison. There was no discussion of its meaning at that time. The Supreme Court in the various cases that have come before it has interpreted it to mean, in a general sense, the right to be treated fairly by government.

The due process clause, as interpreted by the courts, requires:

- that the content of laws passed by legislatures be fair and reasonable. This is called substantive due process.

- that the procedures for conducting hearings and applying and enforcing the law be fair and reasonable. This is called procedural due process.

In this lesson, we will look at the different ways the Supreme Court has interpreted the due process clause when asked to decide whether the content of laws is fair and reasonable. In other words, do the laws place unfair limitations on people's rights to life, liberty, or property?

In the next lesson, we will look at the ways the Supreme Court has used the due process clause to attempt to ensure fairness in the procedures used by the executive and judicial branches in enforcing laws made by the legislatures.

Due process and the protection of property rights

From the 1880s to the 1930s, the Supreme Court used the idea of substantive due process to protect the property rights of citizens from what it considered unreasonable and unfair treatment by state legislatures. The Court's interest focused upon that phrase of the Fourteenth Amendment which says, "nor shall any State deprive any person of . . . property without due process of law." This emphasis, which lasted over fifty years, led to increasing conflicts and finally to important changes in the interpretation of this phrase.

During the late 1880s, there were many serious problems caused by the rapid growth of American industry as large factories and mass production replaced small craftsmen and merchants. The people injured were the farmers and laborers. The farmers' interests were often endangered by large railroad companies which controlled the cost of sending produce to market. The factory workers were often forced to work for long hours, in dangerous conditions, for very low pay. Child labor in factories was common in some states.

To protect the interests of the farmers, laborers, and children, the state legislatures passed a number of laws. Some laws limited the rates the railroad owners could charge farmers for sending their products to market. Other laws required factory owners to improve working conditions, limited working hours, and established minimum wages. Laws were also passed outlawing or regulating child labor.

When the state legislatures passed these laws, they claimed they were promoting the common welfare of the people. Critics disagreed. They thought the best way to promote the common welfare was for government to leave the economy alone. This policy was known by the French phrase, laissez faire. The people who supported laissez faire argued that laws which regulated various forms of economic activity and working conditions did not promote the common welfare, but instead furthered the interests of some groups at the expense of others. The laws, they claimed, protected the interests of farmers and laborers at the cost of violating the property rights of those who owned the railroads and factories.

The Supreme Court from 1880 to 1937 was composed for the most part of justices who considered most social welfare legislation to be unreasonable and unfair limitations on citizens' rights to property. They interpreted the due process clause of the Fourteenth Amendment in a way that found unconstitutional state laws enacted to limit working hours, establish minimum wages, regulate prices, and bar employers from firing workers for belonging to labor unions. For example, in 1905, the Supreme Court declared a New York law unconstitutional because it limited the work week of bakery employees to sixty hours. It claimed that this was an unreasonable limitation on the freedom of contract. The Court consistently found laws that limited people's property rights to be unconstitutional except in situations where it was convinced that the laws were absolutely necessary to protect public health or safety.

Library of Congress

A political cartoon illustrating the anger felt by many at
the Court for allowing child labor

Which should decide what is fair--the courts or the legislatures?

When the Supreme Court decides that a law is unreasonable and unfair and thus unconstitutional, the question is raised as to what is "reasonable" and "fair." The problem is that what one person thinks is reasonable and fair may be considered unreasonable and unfair by another person. Opinions on such matters often depend, at least in part, upon a person's knowledge and experience and upon the person's economic, social, and political views. When the Court makes a decision on such a question, the decision is made by a majority of the nine justices, who have not been elected by the people and who cannot easily be removed from their positions.

In democracies, elected members of government are supposed to be responsible for taking into account people's differing ideas of what is reasonable and fair when they pass and enforce laws that place limitations on your "life, liberty and property" in order to protect the common welfare. Critics of the Supreme Court have often argued that when the Court decides that its interpretation of what is reasonable and fair is correct and that a law passed by a state legislature is unreasonable and unfair, it is acting like a "super legislature." The critics claim that in our system the Congress and state legislatures have the responsibility to decide what the nation's economic policies should be rather than the Supreme Court. As a result of political and economic changes, and new appointments to the Supreme Court, the Court stopped holding laws regulating property rights and the economy unconstitutional under the due process clause.

Problem solving

What is fair and reasonable?

1. Suppose you work to begin your own business, and then hire a number of people to work for you. Your state government has laws which tell you that you cannot ask the people to work more than a certain number of hours and you cannot pay them less than a certain amount per hour. Is this an unreasonable and unfair limitation upon your right to liberty and property? Why?

2. Suppose you are a member of a state legislature that has passed a law protecting children from labor practices the legislature considers abusive, and the Supreme Court says the law unfairly violates the property rights of the employer responsible for such practices. Is this an unreasonable and unfair limitation on your right and obligation to pass laws to promote the general welfare? Why?

Due process and the protection of liberty

During the 1930s, the Supreme Court began to interpret the due process clause of the Fourteenth Amendment in another important way. This change focused on the meaning of the words "nor shall any state deprive any person of . . . liberty . . . without due process of law . . . ." Attention had shifted to concern with the civil liberties of the people.

Since the late 1930s, the word "liberty" in the due process clause of the Fourteenth Amendment has been interpreted by the Supreme Court to include, gradually, almost all the rights guaranteed in the first eight amendments of the Bill of Rights. The process of making these rights apply to state governments is called incorporation. In this process, the various rights contained in the Bill of Rights have been held to be incorporated, one by one, into the Fourteenth Amendment and therefore applicable to the states. Controversy arose, and continues today, over how this section of the due process clause should be interpreted.

What rights should be protected?

Most of the disagreements involve the meaning of the individual rights listed in the Bill of Rights and the extent to which they can be limited by Congress or state legislatures. Like most of the Constitution's clauses, the individual rights listed need to be interpreted. For example, the First Amendment contains the statement that "Congress shall make no law . . . abridging the freedom of speech . . . ." What is meant by "speech"? Is wearing black armbands to protest a war a form of speech? Do laws that prevent people from using loudspeakers to advertise in neighborhoods at night violate free speech? Does the protection of freedom of religion mean that the state cannot control any religious practices?

These are the kinds of questions that arise in deciding whether laws made by federal and state legislatures violate the protections of your rights listed in the Bill of Rights. Ultimately, these questions are decided in the Supreme Court.

Among the rights which have been protected by decisions of the Supreme Court under the due process clause is the right to travel to foreign countries, even though it is not a right specifically listed in the Bill of Rights. The Supreme Court has found laws passed by Congress restricting that right to be unconstitutional. In a 1958 case, Justice William Douglas stated,

The right to travel is a part of the "liberty" of which the citizen cannot be deprived without due process of law under the Fifth Amendment . . . .In Anglo-Saxon law that right was emerging at least as early as the Magna Charta . . . . Freedom of movement across frontiers in either direction, and inside frontiers as well, was a part of our heritage . . . . It may be as close to the heart of the individual as the choice of what he eats, or wears, or reads. Freedom of movement is basic in our scheme of values . . . . Our nation . . . has thrived on the principle that, outside areas of plainly harmful conduct, every American is left to shape his own life as he thinks best, do what he pleases, go where he pleases.

In the next lesson we will deal with procedural due process. Then, in the remaining three lessons of this unit we will deal with the importance of the First Amendment protections of freedom of religion and expression and some of the controversies these rights continue to raise. Here, the Supreme Court still applies the concept of substantive due process when it rules that certain laws limiting freedom of religion and expression are unreasonable and unfair regulations of liberty and therefore unconstitutional.

Reviewing and using the lesson

1. What is the basic purpose of "due process of law"? Distinguish between substantive due process and procedural due process.

2. A factory owner of the late 19th century might think that a state law requiring him to install safety devices was a violation of his rights under the 14th Amendment. Explain how he would support his position.

3. The federal courts often have to choose between "property rights" and the "common welfare" of the people when they decide whether or not a particular law is constitutional. What was the position usually taken by the courts from 1880-1937? Give some examples that illustrate their position.

4. In the late 19th century the courts focused on the word "property" in the 14th amendment. Since the 1930s their attention has shifted to the liberties which may not be denied to Americans by their state governments. What liberties have been protected against state interference by this recent emphasis? Where in the Constitution would you look to find out what these liberties are?

How does procedural due process protect your rights to life, liberty, and property?

Purpose of Lesson 27

As you have learned, the Fifth and Fourteenth Amendments contain protections of your rights under their due process clauses. In the last lesson, you learned that "due process" has been interpreted to mean, in part, that the content of laws must be reasonable and fair. Procedural due process, the subject of this lesson, is the requirement that the procedures used by your federal and state governments be reasonable and fair. The requirements of procedural due process apply in some degree to all of the branches and functions of government. However, in this lesson we will focus specifically on one of their most important applications, that is, to criminal procedures. By showing how these procedural protections might apply to you, we hope to increase your understanding of their importance as part of your rights to life, liberty, and property.

When you have completed this lesson, you should be able to explain the meaning of procedural due process and the reasons for its various protections. Basic ideas and terms included in the lesson which you should be able to explain are listed below.

procedural due process
Fourth Amendment
unreasonable search and seizures
Sixth Amendment
notice clause
assistance of counsel
Fifth Amendment
privilege against self-incrimination
writ of habeas corpus
Eighth Amendment
bail
trial by jury
cruel and unusual punishment
double jeopardy

The importance of procedural due process

The Founders knew that throughout history governments had used their power to enforce criminal laws in ways that had violated the most basic rights of citizens. This was a lesson they had learned from long and painful experience in both England and in the colonies. The criminal law had often been used as a political weapon. This frequently resulted in punishment of the innocent and unfair and inhumane treatment of the guilty. For this reason, they included in the Constitution and the Bill of Rights a number of rights that were specific limitations designed to prevent the possible abuse of power by their government. They were safeguards to protect long-accepted ideas of human freedom, privacy, and dignity from the kinds of attacks they had been subjected to by past governments.

Through the due process clause of the Fourteenth Amendment, most of the procedural protections guaranteed to you by the Constitution and Bill of Rights which originally applied only to the federal government now apply to state governments as well. These protections, taken together, are called procedural due process or due process of law. To understand their importance, let's see how they protect you.

What are your procedural rights and why are they important?

Suppose you are suspected of a crime, arrested, imprisoned while awaiting trial, tried, convicted, and sentenced to prison by a court. What rights are guaranteed to you under the Constitution at each step of that process? How did these rights come to receive the protection of the Constitution? And what is their importance to you and the rest of society? Some of the most important of these rights, their sources, and the reasons they are protected are set forth here.

1. You are suspected of a crime.

Suppose a law-enforcement officer suspects you of having committed a crime. How does the right to due process of law protect you from unfair treatment?

- The Fourth Amendment guarantees that law-enforcement officers cannot search you or your property, arrest you, or take your property unless they can show a good reason for doing so.

This amendment has been interpreted to mean that, except in certain emergencies where they must act quickly, law enforcement officers must get the permission of a judge (in the form of a warrant) to search you or your property, arrest you, or take your property. Further, the judge can only give this permission if the police officer can present reasonable evidence that you may be guilty of a crime, and can describe the evidence being sought. As you can imagine, applying these protections in specific situations can lead to considerable disagreement over such questions as to whether a search or arrest is "reasonable."

The prohibition against unreasonable searches has a long history in English and colonial experience. It dates back to the seventeenth and eighteenth centuries, when judges placed restrictions on the right of police to search people and their homes. The judges had decided this right was necessary when they learned that police had been unreasonable and unfair in searching the homes and meeting places of people with unpopular political and religious beliefs. In the last years of the colonial period, there was public out-cry against searches made by British troops which had been made possible by the detested general warrants known as "writs of assistance." A main purpose of the Fourth Amendment was to place strict limits on the issuing of search warrants by judges.

When the Framers placed the protection against "unreasonable searches and seizures" in the Constitution, they could not know of the technological advances that would allow government agents to engage in search methods such as electronic eavesdropping on conversations.

The Supreme Court has dealt with such changes by interpreting your due process protections to mean that you should be given reasonable protections against government eavesdropping. For example, the Supreme Court has ruled that the police have to get a warrant before they can tap your phone and listen to your conversations.

2. You have been arrested and taken to jail. What are your rights?

- The Sixth Amendment guarantees you the right to know why you have been arrested.

It contains the "notice clause" which says that you must be informed of the "nature and cause of the accusation" for which you have been arrested. The main purpose of this protection is to give you the information necessary to answer the charges and to prepare to defend yourself.

- The Sixth Amendment also guarantees you the right to have a lawyer help you answer the accusation.

It guarantees you the right to the "assistance of counsel" for your defense. If you are like most people, you probably know little about the law, or about the rights you are entitled to while being held in jail, or about court procedures, such as those that deal with examining witnesses. You would be at a great disadvantage trying to answer charges against you even if you were innocent and had been arrested by mistake.

Until about fifty years ago, the right to counsel was interpreted to mean that you were free to hire a lawyer to help you if you wanted one and could afford one. Since that time, the Supreme Court has interpreted the right to counsel to mean that if you are accused of a crime and are too poor to hire a lawyer, the government must provide one at public expense to represent you at all stages of the criminal proceeding.

- The Fifth Amendment guarantees that you have the right to remain silent both at the time of your arrest and throughout your trial.

This right protects you from being forced to give evidence against yourself. It is contained in the "privilege against self-incrimination clause" which says that a person cannot be "compelled in any criminal case to be a witness against himself." The right has its origins in the English common law system dating back at least to the 1500s.

The Framers knew that throughout history it had been common practice to torture people to make them confess to crimes. Even if you were innocent, you might confess to a crime if you were tortured, or given the "third degree." This protection also reflects the belief that even if you were guilty, you should be treated with dignity and not be subjected to cruel and inhumane treatment by your government.

3. You think you have been arrested and are being held in jail unfairly.

Suppose you think that the police have arrested you without having a good reason for doing so, that they are keeping you in jail unfairly, or that they have denied you one of your other basic rights to due process. What can you do?

- Article I, Section 9, of the Constitution guarantees you the right to have a judge hear your story and decide if you are being treated unfairly.

This part of the Constitution guarantees you the protection of the writ of habeas corpus or the "Great Writ of Liberty" as it was known by the Framers. This protection, included in the Magna Carta, has its origins in the English common law and is considered one of the most important safeguards of freedom in the British and American governmental systems. It means that if you are being held in jail, you or someone acting for you, may get an order from a court requiring the police to take you to court so you can argue before a judge that you have been unfairly arrested and should be set free. The police would have to present the evidence they had against you to the judge to justify their actions. If the judge agreed with you, you would be set free. If not, you would be held for trial.

The purpose of the right to habeas corpus is to protect you from being held in jail for a long period of time without being tried and convicted. The Framers knew that it was a common practice for governments to arrest people and put them in jail without ever giving them a fair trial. Today, the writ has also been interpreted to protect you if you have been convicted and are being held in a state or federal prison and can argue that your conviction had been unfairly obtained. It gives you the right to have a judge review your case to see if you have been treated unfairly. It is not guaranteed during times of "rebellion or invasion."

4. You are in jail waiting for your trial.

Suppose after you have been arrested, a judge or a grand jury decides that there is enough evidence that you may be guilty to justify holding you for trial. What rights do you have?

- The Eighth Amendment guarantees the right to be free on reasonable bail while you wait for your trial.

It says that "Excessive bail shall not be required." This idea has a long history in English common law dating back to the Magna Carta. It was a part of the legal tradition that the colonists brought from England. Bail is an amount of money left with the court to guarantee that an accused person will return to court to be tried. It is an attempt to reduce the harm done by imprisonment between arrest and trial. Such imprisonment may punish in advance someone who is eventually found innocent, may cause someone to lose a job or be unable to fulfill family duties, and may make it more difficult to prepare a defense.

The "right to bail" is limited to those who can afford to pay the amount set by the court, which is not considered "excessive" or unreasonable if it is the amount normally charged for a particular offense. If you don't have the money for bail, you may have to remain in jail until your trial. Also, if a judge decides, for example, that you would not show up for your trial or that if you were free you might endanger others, you might be refused the right to be set free on bail.

- The Sixth Amendment guarantees you the right to a speedy and public trial.

This right serves two purposes. First, it protects you from being kept in jail for a long time even though you have not been convicted. Second, it protects you from being tried in secret where members of government might treat you unfairly and no one would ever know about it. The Framers knew that governments had used secret trials to unfairly convict people of crimes for which they probably would not have been convicted in a public trial by a jury of their peers.

5. You are brought to trial. What are your rights in court?

- Article III, Section 2 of the Constitution, and the Sixth Amendment guarantee you the right to a trial by an impartial jury.

The Framers knew that the right to a trial by jury was one of the greatest protections from unfair treatment by the king and his judges that the people of England had developed. In England, the jury was traditionally made up of twelve persons selected from the community at large; they were <u>not</u> members of the government. The purpose of a jury trial is to provide an unprejudiced group to determine the facts and to provide fair judgments about guilt or innocence. Requiring a jury trial is a way of making sure that the criminal justice system is democratic and involves citizens of the community.

- The Sixth Amendment guarantees you the right to be confronted with the witnesses against you.

Suppose a secret informer tells law-enforcement officers that you have committed a crime, but that person is not required to face you and your lawyer in court. You don't know who the person is and have no chance to challenge the accusation. The purpose of this protection is to make sure that you and your lawyer have the chance to face and question anyone who has given evidence against you which may be used to convict you.

- The Sixth Amendment guarantees you the right to compel witnesses in your favor to testify for you.

Suppose you know someone who knows something that might help you with your case, or who even might have evidence to show you are innocent, but the person won't testify for you for one reason or another. As a result, you might be convicted of a crime you didn't commit. This right says that in such situations, the government must do everything it can to bring witnesses who may be in your favor to court to testify for you.

6. You have been convicted of a crime. What rights do you now have?

- The Eighth Amendment guarantees that you may not be subjected to cruel and unusual punishment.

This protection has been interpreted to mean that the punishment shall not be "barbaric." Such punishments as branding or whipping are prohibited. The punishment shall not be "excessive." For example, you cannot be given, as happened in the past, the death sentence for stealing a loaf of bread.

7. You have been tried and found innocent. What rights do you have?

- The Fifth Amendment guarantees you the right to be free from being tried again for the same crime.

The protection against "double jeopardy" is the oldest of the procedural protections that were included in the Constitution. It has its roots in ancient Greek and Roman law, it is in English common law, and it is found in the laws of many nations. It is intended to prevent the government from abusing its power by trying you again and again for the same crime of which you have been found innocent. To allow the government to do this would be to subject you to continued embarrassment, expense, anxiety, and insecurity, and the possibility of eventually being found guilty even though you are innocent. The protection against double jeopardy also protects you, if you have been found guilty, from being punished more than once for the same crime.

Controversies over procedural due process

Controversies over procedural due process have not been over the rightness or wrongness of the basic rights themselves but over how they should be interpreted and applied. The Supreme Court's interpretations of these rights show how it has tried, under changing and often difficult circumstances, to balance your rights as an individual against the responsibility of government to protect all of us from people who break the law and who may endanger our lives, liberty, or property. Since the protection of your individual rights is the main purpose of constitutional government, the problem of balancing these interests is one of the most difficult problems of a limited government.

While controversy remains with regard to the interpretation and extent of particular rights and how they are to be protected, all justices have agreed that fairness in the <u>procedures</u> by which a person is accused and tried for a crime is a cornerstone of our constitutional democracy. The guarantees of procedural fairness or justice are among the most important of your rights contained in the Constitution and Bill of Rights.

Reviewing and using the lesson

1. Make a chart listing Amendments 4, 5, 6, and 8 to the Constitution, which contain guarantees of procedural due process. For each amendment state the right(s) of procedural due process that it protects.

2. What is the right to <u>habeas corpus</u>? Explain why it is one of the most important protections of individual freedom.

3. Are the guarantees of procedural due process outlined in this lesson in the best interests of all citizens or do they make it possible for too many criminals to be set free at the expense of law-abiding citizens? Explain your position.

4. We often hear people say: "Better that nine guilty people go free than one innocent person be convicted." Do you agree? Would you agree if the figures were "ninety-nine" and "one?"

5. Can you think of any circumstances where a defendant might not prefer a jury trial? Explain your answer.

6. Some scholars have said that procedural due process is the "keystone of liberty." Others have called it the "heart of the law." Some scholars have said that the degree of due process protections a nation provides for its citizens is an important indicator of whether the nation has a constitutional government or an autocratic or dictatorial government. Why do you suppose the Founders and these scholars would place such a high value on the protection of the rights of people accused of crimes?

How has your right to freedom of religion been guaranteed?

Purpose of Lesson 28

The importance of freedom of religion to the Founders can be seen by the fact that the first phrase of Amendment I of the Bill of Rights says "Congress shall make <u>no law respecting an establishment of religion, or prohibiting the free exercise thereof;</u>" This and the following lesson will explain the importance of your right to freedom of religion. It will also describe how this right has been applied since the founding of this nation and some of the current controversies about it.

When you complete this lesson, you should be able to describe some of the important events in the history of the relationship between church and state (or government) in the United States. You should also be able to explain some of those reasons why Americans have believed that freedom of religion is one of the most important liberties to be protected by the Constitution. Basic ideas and terms introduced in the lesson which you should be able to explain are listed below.

religious intolerance
establishment of religion
free exercise of religion
"wall of separation"

Religious intolerance and persecution in the early American colonies

The degree of religious freedom that you have today did not exist in Europe, the colonies, or the states formed after the Revolutionary War. Often only one official or "established" religious group was allowed to practice its beliefs. Every subject had to attend its church, obey its requirements, and pay taxes to support it.

Few of the earliest English colonies in North America allowed religious freedom. In fact, in several colonies, especially those in New England, a dominant and intolerant religious group insisted on strict conformity to its own ideas of proper belief and worship.

Dissenters were persecuted. In the early days, some dissenters simply went off into the wilderness and began new colonies of their own. For example, the Reverend Thomas Hooker disagreed with the religious beliefs in Massachusetts. He and his followers left the colony and settled Connecticut. However, their new colony soon became as intolerant in its own way as Massachusetts. The only colonies that tolerated a relatively free expression of religious beliefs and practices were Pennsylvania, Rhode Island, Delaware, and New Jersey.

HOOKER'S EMIGRATION TO CONNECTICUT

Library of Congress

Thomas Hooker seeks religious freedom

By the end of the colonial period, people had become more tolerant of religious differences. Many different religious groups existed together in the same communities and people became used to living and working with others who held different beliefs. In some of the colonies, most notably in New England, many people had become less strict about their own religious beliefs and were more willing to accept different points of view. Consequently, with an increased tolerance of religious differences there came greater demands for genuine religious freedom, which were increasingly made by Quakers, Baptists, Catholics, and others.

There was also widespread opposition to the <u>establishment</u> of one church as the <u>official national church</u>. By the time of the ratification of the Constitution and the Bill of Rights, there was a widely held belief that the federal government should <u>not</u> be allowed to establish an official church for the nation. Many agreed that an established church was harmful to religion and bad for the nation.

Finally, some leaders, notably Thomas Jefferson and James Madison, were greatly concerned about the dangers of religious intolerance. They were well aware that throughout history, religious intolerance had often led to conflict rather than cooperation and to a violation of the basic rights of individuals.

The establishment of religion in the state governments

Even though many of the Founders believed strongly in religious tolerance, a number of the state constitutions deprived members of some religious groups of the rights people who were members of other religious groups had. For example, some states did not allow Catholics or Jews to vote or hold public office. In Massachusetts and Maryland, no one but a Christian was allowed to become governor. For many years, New Hampshire, New Jersey, Massachusetts, and North Carolina required that office holders be Protestants. Even Pennsylvania, which had a bill of rights protecting the "inalienable right of all men to worship God according to the dictates of their own conscience," still disqualified Jews and non-Christians from public office. New York and Virginia were the only states that did not have any restrictions on religious beliefs for persons serving in their state governments.

However, soon after 1776, important changes began to be made in those states in which religion had been established as an official part of the government.

Between 1776 and 1789, New York, Virginia, and North Carolina eliminated state-established religion. Massachusetts, Connecticut, and New Hampshire decided to allow Anglicans and other Protestants to join Congregationalists as a part of the established church. In Maryland, the Constitution written in 1776 gave the legislature the right to tax citizens to support the Christian religion. However, each person was free to decide which denomination should receive his tax money.

The Constitution of South Carolina, written in 1778, said that the Protestant Christian religion was to be the established religion of the state and all Protestant groups would have equal rights and privileges including financial support from tax funds.

These changes meant that in some states there was still an established religion, but it was not just one church or denomination. The established religion, however, was Protestant Christianity. Catholics, Jews, and members of other religions were not entitled to tax support. It was not until 1833 when Massachusetts changed its constitution to separate church and state that the last established religion in the states was eliminated.

Anne Hutchinson was banished from Boston for advocating unpopular religious ideas

The Founders' religious beliefs promote freedom of religion

Most of the Founders were religious people. Despite the history of intolerance, the influence of some of their religious beliefs resulted in promoting the freedom of religion which we have today.

The Founders believed that you have certain natural rights simply because you are a human being. This belief developed in part out of the Puritan idea that God has given you a moral sense and the ability to reason which enables you to tell the difference between what is right and wrong. Philosophers such as John Locke argued that society should allow you to live the way your moral sense, guided by the Bible, tells you is right. The best government, therefore, they believed, is the one that interferes as little as possible with your beliefs, including religious belief, although many did not support tolerance for you if you did not believe in God.

The Founders, it is important to remember, believed that religion is extremely important in developing the kind of character citizens of a free society needed to have in order to remain free. For example, George Washington said in his farewell address that virtue and morality are necessary for a government run by the people. He also believed that morality could not be maintained without religion. At the same time, he joined Thomas Jefferson and James Madison in opposing a bill introduced into the Virginia legislature which would have used tax money to pay for religious teachers.

Madison had been the author of the parts of the Virginia Declaration of Rights, passed in 1776, that provided for freedom of religion. Religion, he insisted, "can be directed only by reason and conviction." Jefferson later wrote the Act for Establishing Religious Freedom which led to the end of an established church in Virginia. Both were acting on the basis of their belief that our right to liberty includes the liberty to believe as our conscience and reason direct. Established churches, they insisted, violate this basic right.

It is clear that the Founders thought religion was an important part of the society. At the same time, they believed strongly that each person has a natural right to his or her own religious beliefs. The separation of the church and state required by the First Amendment is an expression of this belief.

The "establishment" and the "free exercise" clauses

The Framers included two clauses in the First Amendment that protect your religious freedom. These are the establishment clause and the free exercise clause. The establishment clause prohibits the federal government from establishing an official religion for the nation. In the words of Thomas Jefferson, this clause creates a "wall of separation between church and state." However, controversies arise in trying to decide what this separation of church and state should mean. Some people argue that it should be interpreted to mean that the government should have almost nothing to do with religion. This could mean anything from not allowing prayers in public buildings to eliminating tax exemptions for churches and to taking the phrase "In God we trust" off of all money issued by the government. Others argue that the Framers were only opposed to a single national church and the favoring of one religion over another. The next lesson will deal with some of the current controversies over the establishment clause in situations with which you may have first-hand experience. These are issues over religion and the schools.

The free exercise clause protects your freedom to believe or not to believe as well as your freedom, in most cases, to practice your beliefs. For example, if your religion requires you to wear certain kinds of clothing or not to eat certain foods, your freedom to practice these beliefs is protected. In past years, cases involving the free exercise of religious beliefs have involved a wide variety of religious groups such as Mormons, Jehovah's Witnesses, the Amish, and Seventh Day Adventists.

Conflicts between the establishment and free exercise clauses

The problem of protecting religious freedom under the First Amendment is often complicated by the fact that at times there may be a conflict between the establishment clause and the free exercise clause. For example, consider the following problem from a case heard not long ago by the Supreme Court. (*Marsh v. Chambers*, 1983) A state legislature had used tax funds to hire a chaplain to open its sessions with a prayer. This was challenged as being a violation of the establishment clause requiring the separation of church and state. It was defended with the argument that to deny the legislators this right was to violate their right to the free exercise of their religious beliefs.

Article I of the Bill of Rights increased the protection of religious freedom. However, this protection was only from the actions of the federal government, not those of the states. Since there were several state-supported churches, it was generally believed that the First Amendment left the state governments free to support religious groups if they wished to. And some people supported the First Amendment in order to protect the state religious establishments from interference by the federal government.

In the late 1940s, however, the Supreme Court decided two cases that extended the First Amendment's protections of religious liberties against state action by incorporating them under the Fourteenth Amendment's guarantee of liberty. The interpretations of the Constitution in these cases increased the power of the federal courts over state government's activities in the area of religion.

Limitations upon the free exercise of religious beliefs

In 1961, the Supreme Court heard a case involving the state of Maryland. If you had been a citizen of Maryland at that time, you would have had to swear that you believed in God before you could hold a public office. The Supreme Court ruled that this part of Maryland's law violated the protection of freedom of <u>belief</u> guaranteed to every person by the First Amendment. This decision meant that each person has an <u>absolute</u> right to hold any or no religious belief and that no government in the United States has the right to force anyone to accept any religious beliefs or to censor such beliefs.

However, while you have the right to hold any religious belief you wish, this does not mean that the federal government or state governments cannot make and enforce laws controlling your religious <u>practices</u>. Religious practices may be limited if they offend public morals, jeopardize public health, or in other ways endanger the common welfare. For example, according to court rulings, religious practices involving polygamy or handling rattlesnakes may be forbidden without violating citizens' constitutional rights. Couples who wish to marry may be required by state law to take blood tests before being given a marriage license. Children may be required to be vaccinated for small pox before being admitted to school, even if these requirements violate their religious beliefs.

Reviewing and using the lesson

1. The First Amendment forbids both an "establishment of religion" and any attempt by government at "prohibiting the free exercise [of religion]." Distinguish between these two prohibitions. Select laws or practices from history which would not be permissible under the First Amendment.

2. List some colonial or early state laws which show what an "established" religion is.

3. Why didn't the First Amendment apply to actions of state governments before 1940?

4. Why would the First Amendment provide individuals an absolute right to freedom of belief, but allow the government to limit the practices of one's religious beliefs? How is this related to the natural rights philosophy and the purposes of our constitutional government?

Why are there continuing controversies over religion and education?

As this 19th century political cartoon illustrates, most Americans believed strongly in the separation of church and state

Purpose of Lesson 29

Thomas Jefferson's position that there should be a "wall of separation" between church and state has been criticized by the leaders of some religious groups and strongly supported by others. This has been especially true in the sensitive area of education. In this lesson, we are going to examine some of the issues that arise regarding the relationship between religion and education and the ways in which they have been resolved by the Supreme Court. This should help you to understand the deeply divided opinions that

Americans have on the meaning of religious freedom, and the range of positions on the topic.

When you have completed this lesson, you should be able to describe the criteria that have been used by the Supreme Court in determining the constitutionality of laws affecting the relationship between religion and the schools. You should also be able to explain the issues raised and the opinions of the Court in several leading cases. And, finally, you should be able to apply your understanding of the First Amendment to specific situations.

Until recently, prayer in public schools was a common practice in many areas

Problem solving

To help you understand some of the current controversies over religion and education, we have included below some of the important questions that are presently being debated. We have also included guidelines for making decisions about these questions that were developed by Chief Justice Warren E. Burger who wrote the majority opinion in a 1971 case involving the establishment clause of the First Amendment. This test is known as the "Lemon test" since it was first written in a case called *Lemon v. Kurtzman* (1971). According to this test, for a law involving religion in the schools to avoid violating the Constitution it must satisfy the following requirements.

1. The primary purpose of a law must be <u>secular</u>, not religious. This means it must not have a religious purpose.

2. The principal or primary effect of the law must not be to advance or inhibit religion.

3. The law must not create an excessive government entanglement with religion.

How would you decide these issues regarding religion and the schools?

Each of the following situations involves a law that might be considered a violation of the <u>establishment clause</u> of the First Amendment. Read them and use the three-part test you have just read to decide if you

think the laws should be declared unconstitutional. To accomplish this task, it may be helpful for your class to be divided into groups. Each group should be assigned several of the following situations. Decisions made by the groups should be reported to the full class for discussion.

1. Your state passes a law which allows your public school to have a daily one-minute period for silent prayer or meditation.

2. Your state passes a law which requires the textbooks used in your public school science or biology classes which discuss the theory of evolution to include a balanced treatment of creation science.

3. Your state passes a law requiring your public school principal to post a copy of the Ten Commandments in every classroom.

4. Your state passes a law which gives parents who send their children to either public or parochial schools a tax deduction for tuition, transportation, and educational materials.

5. Your state has a policy which allows your public school's algebra teacher to spend a part of the work day at a parochial school giving remedial instruction to underachieving students.

Deciding contemporary issues about religion and education

At the time the Constitution was written, public schools as we know them did not exist. Children who attended school usually received an education which included some degree of religious teaching. As public education became more important and widespread in the nation, sharp controversies over the extent to which religious teaching and practices should be supported in the public schools began to arise.

The following are questions regarding the relationship between religion and the public schools that have been dealt with in Supreme Court cases since 1925.

1. Should federal or state tax money be used to support private religious schools?

The state government of Louisiana provides free textbooks for all students in parochial and public schools. In 1930, the Supreme Court decided this did not violate the "establishment" clause and was constitutional because it was an aid to school children rather than public assistance to church schools. (*Cochran v. Louisiana State Board of Education*, 1930)

A New Jersey case involved a similar question. New Jersey at one time provided free bus transportation for school children traveling to either parochial or public schools. The Supreme Court, in a five-to-four decision in 1947, declared this law constitutional on the ground that it provided for public safety. (*Everson v. Board of Education of Ewing Township*, 1947) Nevertheless, the Court declared the following principle, which has dominated constitutional decisions for most of the past 40 years. It declared that the First Amendment applies not only to the federal government but to state governments as well (by incorporation through the meaning of "liberty" in the Fourteenth Amendment):

> The establishment of religion clause of the First Amendment means at least this: Neither a state nor the federal government can set up a church. Neither can pass laws which aid one religion, aid all religions, or prefer one religion over another . . . . No tax in any amount, large or small, can be levied to support any religious activities or institutions, whatever they may be called, or whatever form they may adopt to teach or practice religion.

2. Should public schools provide certain periods of "released time" during the day when students can attend special classes to receive religious instruction from their own minister, priest, or rabbi?

"Released time" means that students in public schools are released during a part of the normal school day to attend special classes where they are given religious instruction.

In 1940, members of the three largest religious groups in the United States--Roman Catholic, Protestant, and Jewish--joined together in Champaign, Illinois, to provide for the religious instruction of school children. Classes were held in the regular public school classrooms. Separate groups were taught by Protestant ministers, Roman Catholic priests, and Jewish rabbis. Students attended only with the consent of their parents, and those who did not choose to take religious instruction were required to stay in study rooms.

Mrs. Vashti McCollum, a parent, brought suit because she did not wish her child to be given religious teaching, nor did she wish him to be embarrassed because he was not receiving such instruction.

In a 1948 ruling, the Supreme Court ruled in favor of Mrs. McCollum, saying that a state may not use its public school system to promote religious education even though it aided all religions. Justice Hugo Black, speaking for the Court, based the decision on the Everson opinion. (*McCollum v. Board of Education*, 1948)

The *Everson* and *McCollum* cases stirred wide debate among interested church groups. It also led to debate among scholars, some of whom felt that the Court had gone well beyond the intent of the First Amendment.

Four years after the *McCollum* decision, the Court heard a case in which the New York public schools were releasing students during the school day, on parental request only, to go to religious centers for instruction. Those who were not released remained in the classrooms. No religious instruction was offered in the public school buildings.

Justice William O. Douglas, while supporting the idea of the separation of church and state, nevertheless upheld the New York system, in which "the public schools do no more than accommodate their schedules to a program of outside religious instruction . . . . We cannot read into the Bill of Rights . . . a philosophy of hostility to religion." (*Zorach v. Clausen*, 1952)

3. Should schools require students to take part in prayers or the reading of the Bible during regular public school hours?

Some time ago, the New York State Board of Regents required a prayer as a daily exercise in New York public schools. The prayer was "non-denominational," written by state officials, and students who did not wish to participate in the exercise were permitted to remain silent or to be excused from the schoolroom.

In 1962 the Supreme Court held that the prayer required by the New York Board of Regents was unconstitutional. (*Engel v. Vitale*, 1962) The Court held that such an officially established prayer program violated the "establishment of religion" clause of the First Amendment.

The State of Pennsylvania had a law which called for "at least ten verses from the Holy Bible to be read without comment, at the opening of each public school on each school day." Any child was excused from the exercise upon written request of his parent or guardian.

In 1963, the Supreme Court declared this law an unconstitutional establishment of religion. The Court said that the "establishment of religion" and "free exercise" clauses of the First Amendment require the government to be strictly neutral in matters of religion, "protecting all, preferring none, disparaging none." (*Abington School District v. Schempp*, 1963)

In 1985, the Supreme Court declared unconstitutional an Alabama law that required a period of silence "for meditation or voluntary prayer in public schools." (*Wallace v. Jaffree*, 1985)

Problem solving

What position would you take?

1. Select any one of the above cases and explain the basic questions involved. Then take and defend a position on the questions.

2. For the case you have selected, explain any conflicts it may involve in the application of the principles of the natural rights philosophy, representative democracy, and constitutional government.

The controversy continues

The Supreme Court's decisions in the school prayer cases have stirred heated controversy in the press, among church groups, in Congress, and in state legislatures. Some religious organizations have been strongly in favor of adding an amendment to the Constitution which would take away the Supreme Court's power to review state legislation regarding religious practices in the public schools. They argue this is necessary so that school children will not be deprived of their religious heritage or denied moral instruction.

On the other hand, spokespersons of the major religious groups have generally supported the Supreme Court's position that government should be neutral with respect to religious activities. The separation of church and state, they point out, does not prevent people from praying at any time or going to the church of their choice.

Reviewing and using the lesson

1. Do you support a proposed constitutional amendment permitting voluntary prayer in the public schools? Why?

2. Should biology teachers in the public schools be required to present the Biblical theory of creation as an alternative to the theory of evolution by natural selection? Why?

3. Should the public schools be permitted to close in observance of Christmas and Easter? Why?

4. Should pre-game silent prayers by public school athletic teams be discontinued? Why?

5. What responsibilities accompany your right to religious freedom? Explain what they are and why you believe you have them.

What is the importance of your right to freedom of expression?

Exercising their right of free speech and free assembly, thousands join Martin Luther King, Jr., in a demonstration in 1963

UPI/Bettmann Newsphoto

Purpose of Lesson 30

The Founders placed great importance upon freedom of expression. Under the First and the Fourteenth Amendments, neither federal nor state governments can place unreasonable or unfair limitations upon this right. This means that there are very few situations in which the government can interfere with your right to

- discuss anything you wish

- write, publish, or read anything you wish

- gather together to associate with whomever you wish

- petition your government to correct wrongs

This lesson provides you with an introduction to some of the major issues raised by the question of freedom of expression. You will learn about some of the historical events which help us to understand why the right to freedom of expression was so important that it required the protection of the First Amendment to the Constitution. You will also learn some of the principal arguments in support of freedom of expression. Criteria are introduced that are used to determine when it is reasonable and fair to limit freedom of expression in favor of other important values and interests. Finally, you will read about some of the important cases the Supreme Court has decided in this area.

When you have completed this lesson, you should be able to explain the importance of freedom of expression, both to the individual and to the preservation and improvement of constitutional democracy. You should also be able to explain situations in which it is reasonable and fair to place limitations upon this freedom, and the criteria that may be used to do so. Basic ideas and terms introduced in the lesson which you should be able to explain are listed below.

> **sedition**
> **clear and present danger test**
> **incitement test**
> **dangerous tendency test**
> **free market place of ideas**
> **advocate**

The Founders, history, and freedom of expression

The importance the Founders placed on your right to freedom of expression is made evident by the following phrases in the First Amendment to the Constitution.

> Congress shall make no law . . . abridging the freedom of speech, or of the press; or the right of the people peaceably to assemble, and to petition the Government for a redress of grievances.

It is not surprising that the Founders placed so much importance upon freedom of expression, given their experiences and knowledge of history. They knew that attempts to restrict freedom of expression had often occurred in the past in order to limit the people's access to ideas and information. For example:

- In England, about 1600 A.D., there were laws that required all people to believe in the same religious doctrines. People opposed to these laws spoke, wrote, and distributed materials criticizing them. Members of the government knew that one of the best ways to stop these dissenters from spreading their ideas was to limit their right to print and distribute them. So they passed laws which said that all printing in England could only be done in three cities, and that before being printed, all books had to be approved by the Archbishop of Canterbury and the Bishop of London.

- In 1682, in the Colony of Virginia, a printer named John Buckner was accused of printing the laws of the colony without the governor's permission. The next year the governor made a law that no person in the colony would ever be allowed to use a printing press. The governor said, "Printing has encouraged [the people] to learn and even criticize the best governments. God keep us from free schools and printing."

- In the colony of New York, in 1735, a newspaperman named John Peter Zenger wrote in his newspaper that the governor had rigged elections, that his officials were incompetent, and that the colony was in danger of becoming a dictatorship. The governor had Zenger arrested and brought to trial for making these criticisms. After a lengthy trial, the jury decided that since Zenger's charges against the governor were true, he should be set free.

In some cases, repression of freedom of expression had tragic results. The following are notable examples from ancient history and the colonial period.

- In ancient Athens, in the year 399 B.C., the great philosopher Socrates was accused of corrupting the youth with his teaching. Athenian judges warned Socrates that unless he agreed to stop teaching, they would order his execution. In response, Socrates replied that no official could order him what to think or what to teach--he answered to a higher authority. As a result, he was condemned to death.

- In colonial Massachusetts, in the year 1660, Mary Dyer taught that all men and women were equal before God, and that slavery, war, and capital punishment were evil. She was hanged by the Puritans in the city of Boston for preaching beliefs that were different from those of other members of the colony.

Why is freedom of expression important?

In addition to their knowledge of history, the Founders believed in natural rights and representative democracy. They believed that your right to hold and express your beliefs is one of your "inalienable rights" that is crucial if you are to be able to be a responsible and capable citizen. Several of the most important reasons why this right is so important are set forth below.

1. Individual development and human dignity

Your right to develop, hold, and express ideas is an important part of your intellectual, moral, and social development. So, of course, is your right to hear and consider the views of others. Further, a respect for your dignity and abilities requires your having the right to gain knowledge and express your beliefs and opinions.

2. Truth and progress

It is through the free competition of different ideas and beliefs that the truth is most likely to be found. As Justice Oliver Wendell Holmes, Jr., put the argument, "The best test of truth is the power of the thought to get itself accepted in the competition of the market." Scientific discoveries and intellectual developments seem more likely to come about when it is possible for ideas to be discussed and debated freely.

In the "free marketplace of ideas," all points of view, even those with which you may disagree, have the right to be heard, and it is important to hear them.

3. The maintenance of representative democracy

The ultimate power of our government is with you and the rest of the people. If you are to judge wisely and to make informed choices about candidates and policies, you must be able to get the information you need and be able to discuss it freely. Freedom of expression is also important in providing a way for you to check on how well members of government are doing their jobs and to let them know if you approve or disapprove of their actions.

4. Providing a "safety-valve"

Having the right to express yourself freely gives you an opportunity to "blow off steam." You may be more willing to accept decisions made by government if you have at least had a fair opportunity to be heard and to participate in the decision-making process. You may also be more willing to use democratic means of attempting to influence your government rather than resorting to violence.

5. The protection of life, liberty, and property

The lessons of history are clear, that when governments gain the power to place unreasonable and unfair limitations upon your freedom of expression, they become arbitrary and despotic, violate basic principles of justice, and deprive you of fundamental human rights.

The importance of freedom of expression to the protection of all of your rights and of our free society itself has led scholars and justices to say it should be protected more carefully than many of your other basic rights. The Supreme Court has held, as you will learn, that freedom of expression can only be limited when it very clearly endangers other important values and interests.

When should your freedom of expression be limited?

Although the First Amendment appears to say that there cannot be <u>any</u> laws limiting your right to freedom of expression, this does not mean that you can freely say absolutely anything. For example, you do not have the right falsely to shout "Fire!" in a crowded theater because you might cause a panic in which people could be injured or killed. You do not have a

right to tell military secrets to foreign nations because of the requirement of national security, that is, our need to protect our entire nation.

Given our strong belief that our right to express ourselves on political matters is vital to the preservation and improvement of our constitutional democracy, you can imagine the problems that arise when decisions have to be made about when it is reasonable and fair for the government to limit this freedom. Most people, including the Supreme Court, believe that your right to freedom of expression must be balanced against other important values and interests of our society such as public safety or national security. This means that your right to express yourself freely may be limited in certain situations if it would seriously endanger other very important values and interests.

For example, suppose you try to convince other people to rise up and overthrow our government by violent means such as the Founders used to overthrow the British government. And, suppose you believe that our government should be replaced with one which severely restricts those basic rights this nation was founded to protect. Under what conditions do you think your government should be able to arrest, try, and convict you for expressing such beliefs?

Problem solving

Tests used in limiting freedom of expression

Over the years the Supreme Court has developed different guidelines or "tests" to use in deciding when it is reasonable and fair to limit freedom of expression. We will study three of these tests used in only one of the many types of situations that occur regarding freedom of expression.

The following three tests have been developed by the Supreme Court at different periods to decide when freedom of expression may be limited in situations or cases that involve what is called <u>sedition</u>. These are situations in which a person tries to convince others to engage in the overthrow of our government. Read these tests and be prepared to apply them to the cases that follow which involve issues of sedition.

1. The **clear and present danger test.** The government may limit your freedom of expression if its result is that people will break the law so soon after you have expressed your ideas that there will be no opportunity for full discussion of the consequences of what you are suggesting.

119

2. The **dangerous tendency test**. The government may limit your freedom of expression if it creates a dangerous tendency among others to break a law. The government does not have to wait until an unlawful act is about to happen.

3. The **incitement test**. The government may limit your freedom of expression if it can show that your speech is directed to inciting or producing immediate unlawful action and is likely to cause that action to happen.

Applying the tests to sedition cases

To help you understand the problems in deciding under what conditions the government should be allowed to limit your freedom of expression, the following exercise is provided for you to complete in small groups.

Each group should be assigned to read one of the following cases. Then, try to reach a decision on the following questions on the case to which the group has been assigned.

1. Should the person in the case have his or her right to freedom of expression limited?

2. Which of the three tests you have just studied should be used to decide the case? Be prepared to explain why you have made your decision.

3. Explain which of the tests seem to provide more and which less protection of your right to freedom of expression.

Case No. 1: *Schenck v. the United States* (1919)

In 1917, the United States was involved in World War I. Congress passed the Federal Espionage Act which made it unlawful to make statements intended to interfere with the armed forces of the United States or to obstruct the recruitment or enlistment of personnel in the armed forces.

Charles Schenck, the general secretary of the Socialist Party during World War I, was against the United States entering the war. He sent out letters to about 15,000 young men eligible to be drafted into the army. The letters strongly stated Schenck's opinion that the war was only being fought in the interests of the rich people in our country and that the federal government did not have the right to draft men to be in the army. Schenck encouraged the men to speak out and try to get the draft laws repealed.

Schenck was arrested on the grounds that his letters would tend to make people disobey the laws even though his letters didn't actually recommend this. He was tried, convicted, and imprisoned. He appealed his case to the Supreme Court claiming that the Federal Espionage Act was a violation of his First Amendment right to freedom of expression.

Case No. 2: *Gitlow v. New York* (1925)

During World War I, some of the Russian people revolted against the Czar and overthrew the government. The leaders who finally took over were Communists who believed the workers of all countries should also take over their governments. During the 1920s there was evidence that some Communists in the United States wished to overthrow the government by force. In New York, a man named Gitlow printed a Communist pamphlet and sent 16,000 copies through the mails to people in this country. The pamphlet said that the workers of the United States should begin a Communist revolution, have large strikes, and destroy the United States form of government.

Gitlow was arrested under the 1902 New York Criminal Anarchy Law that made it a crime to advocate the violent overthrow of the government. He was tried, convicted, and imprisoned. He appealed his case to the Supreme Court. He claimed that his right to freedom of expression had been unfairly limited because there was no evidence that his pamphlets had made anyone break the law.

Case No. 3: *Dennis v. United States* (1951)

In 1940, Congress passed a law known as the Smith Act which made it illegal to teach or print materials advocating the overthrow of the government of the United States by force or violence. In 1948, with Soviet-American tensions rising, the government began prosecution under the Smith Act against Eugene Dennis and ten others. Dennis was secretary general of the Communist Party of the United States. He and the others were charged with conspiring to form groups to teach the overthrow of the government by force and violence. They were tried, convicted, and imprisoned. They appealed to the Supreme Court claiming that the Smith Act violated their rights to freedom of speech, of the press, and of association.

Case No. 4: *Yates v. United States* (1957)

In 1951, fourteen members of the Communist Party in California were arrested for violation of the Smith Act. This act made it illegal to teach or print materials advocating the overthrow of the government of the United States by force or violence. The government accused the Communists of writing and publishing articles and conducting schools which promoted the overthrow of the government, in violation of the Smith Act. All fourteen persons were arrested, tried, convicted, and sentenced to prison for five years. They appealed their case to the Supreme Court claiming that the law violated their freedom of expression.

Case No. 5: *Brandenburg v. Ohio* (1969)

A local leader of the Ku Klux Klan spoke at a rally of the Klan held on a farm in Ohio. The rally was attended by twelve members of the Klan and a reporter and cameraman from a local television station. The film showed the twelve persons carrying guns gathered around a burning cross. The leader told the group that if the federal government continued to suppress the white race ". . . there might have to be some revenge taken. We are marching on Congress July the 4th, four hundred thousand strong." He was arrested and convicted under a 1919 Ohio law which prohibited unlawful means of terrorism as a means of accomplishing political reform. He was tried, convicted, and sentenced to ten years in prison. He appealed his case to the Supreme Court claiming that the Ohio law violated his right to freedom of expression.

Other issues of freedom of expression

All of the issues raised by the First Amendment protection of freedom of expression have not been raised in this lesson. We have not dealt, for example, with many of the important questions of free speech and public safety, freedom of the press and fair trials, and freedom of association. We have, however, attempted to convey some idea of the importance of freedom of expression as well as some of the problems of balancing this freedom with other important values and interests.

Clearly, your right to be free to express your views is one of the most important of those inalienable rights of which Jefferson spoke. As with other rights, it implies a corresponding duty: the recognition and zealous devotion to the protection of the same right for others, even for those with whom you disagree.

Reviewing and using the lesson

1. What arguments did the Founders use to support their claim that freedom of expression is a necessity in a free society?

2. Some scholars and judges believe that the First Amendment guarantees of freedom of speech and expression are absolute. This would mean that there may be no prohibitions against any form of expression. Others think that some restrictions are permitted if required by important interests of our society, provided these limitations are necessary and reasonable. With which position do you agree? Why?

3. Suppose a person who was running for the presidency of the United States openly stated that, if elected, he would deny First Amendment rights to those who opposed his policies. (For the sake of discussion, assume he has a real chance of being elected and carrying out his threat.) Should his right to free speech be denied? Why?

4. Should a speaker who calls for violent action be protected by the First Amendment while a member of his audience who responds to his words is sent to prison? Why?

Unit Six: Responsibilities of the Citizen

Collection of the Boatmen's National Bank of St. Louis

In this 19th century painting, voters listen to a political candidate.
Informed citizens are necessary for constitutional democracy to work.

Purpose of Unit Six

We have studied the basic ideas of our constitutional democracy. Up to this point, most of our attention has been paid to examining the role of the government. We now turn to a question that is of equal or greater importance. What is the role of the citizen? We will not attempt to answer this question for you since the answer is one you must arrive at yourself. However, in this final lesson we will set forth some of the important questions and considerations that should be taken into account in arriving at an answer.

What should be the responsibilities of the citizen?

Purpose of Lesson 31

It is your right to decide what responsibilities you think you should undertake as a citizen. In making this decision, it is useful to consider what you have learned about constitutional government and our nation's history. It is also useful to consider such topics as the purposes of our government, participation, the responsibilities that accompany our basic rights, and the sources of those responsibilities. This lesson will provide you with an opportunity to examine these and other important topics related to the question of the responsibilities of the citizen.

When you finish this lesson, you should have a better understanding of the roles a citizen may take in our constitutional democracy. You should also be able to explain the following terms.

citizen
alien
politics

What is the purpose of our government?

In the previous lessons of this book, we have studied the basic ideas underlying the political system of the United States. We started out by asking why the people who set up the first governments in this country thought we needed government at all. We learned of their belief that the main reason it is better to have a government than to live without one is to protect our basic rights.

Some people have thought that government was needed for other reasons. For example, some have thought we needed government to help us become good people who fully developed those intellectual and moral qualities that make us human. But most Americans have agreed with the position of the Founders and the natural rights philosophers. That position was that the main purpose of government is to protect our basic rights to life, liberty, and property, and to pursue happiness as we understand it.

What kind of government is best suited to fulfilling this purpose?

Americans have also believed that the kind of government that is most likely to protect these rights rather than violate them is one that is based on consent. In addition we have believed in limited government, that is to say, constitutional government. We have learned that in a constitutional government the purpose of a constitution is to establish a law above the government which imposes limitations on that government. There are certain things a constitutional government is prohibited from doing, such as placing unreasonable and unfair limitations on our rights to freedom of religion and expression.

We have also discussed another important ideal in which Americans have believed. That was the ideal of republican government. You will remember the Founders' belief that the purpose of a republican government was to promote the common welfare of its citizens, who governed themselves with the assistance of elected representatives.

Constitutionalism, natural rights, and republicanism are the major ideas underlying the American political system. We are now going to examine various views on the responsibilities of citizenship in such a system. But first, we must distinguish a citizen from a non-citizen.

Who is a citizen?

In our country, anyone who is born in the United States or is born to citizens of the United States, is a citizen. People who are not citizens are aliens. By satisfying certain requirements, aliens may become citizens.

Both citizens and aliens who live in the United States must obey the laws of the United States. They also receive the protection of those laws. Aliens are guaranteed most of the rights given to citizens. If they are tried in a court of law, for example, they are guaranteed the same rights to due process that are provided in the Constitution for citizens.

There is one very important right, however, which citizens have and aliens do not: the right to participate in the government. This right includes the right to vote and to hold public office. This, many people have argued, is what distinguishes the citizen from the non-citizen. Some people would also argue that, in addition to possessing this important right, citizens also have special responsibilities toward their country which non-citizens do not. Before examining what those responsibilities might be, we will first discuss the right to participate in the politics of the United States.

What is participation?

All American citizens, with very few exceptions, possess the right to participate in the political life of the country. Voting for candidates and running for public office are two examples which are most obvious. But are there other ways of participating? What about working on the campaign of a candidate you think should be elected? If you contribute money to a candidate you are certainly participating. Writing letters to public officials, reading newspapers, talking about public issues with your friends, and going to meetings where political questions are discussed, are all ways in which the citizens participate in the political life of their country.

When we see how many different ways there are of participating, we understand that we could spend a large part of our lives on politics and government. How can we decide how much of our time we should spend on such matters?

Should you participate?

As you probably know, many citizens in our country either do not participate in our political system or do so very infrequently. At the same time, you have probably heard people argue that all citizens have the responsibility to participate. The decision about whether or not you should participate is an important one for you to make.

In making your decision about whether you should participate, it is helpful to answer the question of why we think we need government in the first place. As we have seen, the Framers and most Americans have agreed that the purpose of government is to protect your life, liberty, and property.

If you think the purpose of government is to protect your rights, why should you participate? Why should you vote for representatives, inform yourself of

their qualifications, and keep up with what your government is doing?

Wouldn't we do these things for the same reasons that we would want to keep an eye on anyone we hired to do a job for us? If we hire someone to clean our house, or if we hire a dentist to fix our teeth, or a mechanic to repair our car, or a teacher to teach our children, we want to make certain that these people can do the things we hire them to do, and that they do them. In other words, we want to look into their qualifications for the job, and we will certainly check on how they are doing that job so we can decide whether we want to keep them.

In our nation, the people working in our government are public servants. We, the people, have given them their jobs. And their jobs affect our lives, liberty, and property. Considering the importance of these responsibilities, it seems reasonable that we should pay at least as much attention to how they are fulfilling their responsibilities as we would to someone who was repairing our car or our plumbing. For this reason alone, one might argue that it is wise to participate. We participate to ensure that the government does what it is supposed to do. In short, if we participate, we do so because it is in our interest to do so.

How much time should you spend in participating?

But how much time should we spend participating? If it seems that everything is going as we think it should, we will probably decide that we don't have to spend too much time checking up on the people we hire to do things for us, although we would probably be foolish to ignore them completely. And so it is with the government and the people who work there: the president, senators, representatives, and judges, as well as the many civil servants who are part of the bureaucracy of the government. As long as we are more or less satisfied with the way they are doing their job, we probably will not wish to spend too much time checking up on them, although we will want to keep an eye on them. This is especially true because of the importance for us of the things they do.

When should you keep a "close eye" on government?

As we have seen, the natural rights philosophers did not think that the government should be responsible for taking care of all of the most important things in life, but they did think that what it does do--protect

124

our natural rights--is pretty important. If we look at the government and what it ought to do from this point of view, we obviously will be very concerned that it do those things we expect of it. We certainly expect that it will protect our rights.

If we have reason to suppose that instead of protecting our rights it is violating them, we are only doing the sensible thing to keep a closer eye on government. If we believe that the government is not providing the security we think it is supposed to provide, we will want to find out why and find ways to improve the situation. This may involve hiring different people to work in the government. For example, we may elect different people to represent us and make the laws on our behalf. If the matter is very important and we are seriously dissatisfied with the performance of those who are working for us in the government, we may want to do more than simply vote. We may want to donate money to a political campaign or work for a candidate we think will do a better job.

What responsibilities accompany our basic rights?

We believe that the protection of our basic rights by our government is what makes our nation so much better to live in than dictatorships and other non-constitutional regimes which have existed throughout history. But being a citizen in such a system means more than just having, exercising, and protecting our basic rights. We Americans have often been criticized for being so concerned with protecting our rights that we have forgotten the responsibilities that accompany them. There are few rights, if any, that can exist for long in a society unless people fulfill the responsibilities that go along with them.

We may disagree on what many of these responsibilities are, but there is a great deal of agreement with regard to some of them. For example, most people will agree that if you wish to attend a meeting and to exercise your right to speak freely, you should fulfill the responsibility of respecting other people's right to do the same. If you disrupt the meeting and deny others the right to speak, it is reasonable and fair to exclude you and deny you the right to speak there. If you ignore others' rights, you may have to give up your own. Some responsibilities are enforced by law. For example, if you violate another person's right to property, you may give up your own right to freedom and be put in jail.

What is the source of the responsibilities of the citizen?

But what is the source of the responsibilities we must fulfill in order to protect our rights? Do we have these responsibilities only because many of them are written into the law? If this were true, there would be little difference between constitutional democracy and dictatorship.

In our political tradition, the responsibilities that accompany our basic rights are considered to be based on our consent to be governed. If we choose to live among others in a society, we give our consent to be governed by certain basic rules of that society. We have entered into an agreement with the other members of the society to take the responsibility of obeying its rules.

Must you obey bad rules?

But what if you disagree with some of the rules of your society or think they are wrong? In our system of government, you have a right to try to have them changed. But until you get them changed, you will be held responsible for obeying the laws.

But are we required always to obey the law? Here we face an old problem. What should you do when your government requires you to do something that conflicts strongly with your moral or religious beliefs?

If you decide you want to take on the responsibility of being a citizen, you may be faced with a conflict between the requirements of citizenship and the demands of morality. This problem has been with us since at least the time of the ancient Greeks 2,500 years ago. For example, Socrates argued that his responsibilities to his philosophy and the search for truth were more important than his responsibilities as a citizen to obey the laws of the government of Athens.

If you try to be a completely good person you can only promise unlimited obedience to a completely good government. But in real life, no government is perfect. For this reason many people argue that there are limits to our consent to obey government. They do not believe that our political responsibilities are absolute or unlimited.

What should you do when your government does something that conflicts strongly with your conscience or religious beliefs? In extreme cases, some people have chosen to obey their conscience rather than obey what they believed to be unjust laws.

In the 1800s, the writer and philosopher Henry David Thoreau went to jail for refusing to pay taxes in protest against slavery and the Mexican-American War of 1846. More recently, in the 1950s and 1960s, Dr. Martin Luther King, Jr., and others chose to go to jail as a way of protesting and challenging the racial segregation laws then existing. This kind of conflict often arises during wartime when citizens opposed to war are called upon to serve in the armed forces.

What choices do you have if you think a law is unjust?

It is important to understand that choosing to disobey your government when your moral or religious beliefs are in conflict with the law is an extreme choice. Usually there are lawful and less dramatic ways in which you can express your position and try to influence your government's decisions.

Voting for people who believe as you do and writing letters to public officials and the news media are common methods of getting laws changed. Some people organize groups, write leaflets and pamphlets, circulate petitions, speak in public, and participate in peaceful demonstrations as a means of changing governmental policies.

Such forms of participation are commonly used by democratic citizens whose feelings of injustice have been aroused and who want to work to set things right. They are the most usual ways for you to express your agreement or disagreement with your government's actions. They are also often the most appropriate and the most effective ways to influence members of your government.

What is the importance of the common welfare?

We have seen that one of the most important ideas in republicanism is the idea of the common welfare. In Lesson 3, we learned that some of the philosophers who wrote about republican government argued that it differed from other kinds of government because its goal is the achievement of the common welfare. Moreover, they believed that republican government is possible only when the citizens possess civic virtue, that is, when they prefer the common welfare to their own personal interests.

We have also seen that the ideal of republican government was held by the Framers of the Constitution. Given this ideal, it is worth asking what the common welfare is.

How can you determine the common welfare?

In some situations, the common welfare may be quite clear. Most of us will agree that our welfare depends upon our being protected from criminals, foreign enemies, or the pollution of the air or water. But in other situations, we may disagree, no matter how intelligent, well-informed, and well-intentioned we may be. For example, there is great disagreement about whether protective tariffs, price supports for farm products, compulsory public service, or our present tax system promote the common welfare.

The problem of determining the common welfare and suggesting that you should sometimes give up your personal interests to promote it raises several important questions. Some of these are set forth below to help you understand the difficulties of this issue. Discuss your answers with others in your class. If you find it difficult to reach agreement on the answers, don't be concerned--you are not alone.

Problem solving

1. Is the common welfare the "greatest happiness of the greatest number of people"? If so, what does this mean?

2. Is the common welfare what is good for 50 percent of the people plus one, for example, or of 95 percent?

3. Is the common welfare the goals that all people in the nation share? If so, how do we find out what those goals are?

4. Why should people in the minority prefer the common welfare when it conflicts with their personal interests and needs?

When should you consider the interests of others more important than your own?

If you decide to take your role as a citizen seriously and to participate in our political system, you will often be faced with decisions that involve a conflict between your personal needs and interests, those of other people, and the common welfare. What position should you take?

Problem solving

1. If you can't agree upon what is in the common welfare, should you just pursue your own interests without thinking of the common welfare or at least of some of the interests of other people? Why?

2. Even if you can't agree on the common welfare, should you at least try to consider others' interests along with your own when you participate in making decisions that affect them? Why?

What do you think your responsibilities as a citizen should be?

We have discussed some of the considerations useful to think about in deciding what responsibilities citizens should undertake in our society. Other considerations may occur to you in the course of your studies and discussions. And, of course, we will differ in our answers to some of the questions of responsibility raised or implied in this lesson.

We conclude this text with several quotations for you to consider and discuss. They contain important ideas to take into account in deciding what our responsibilities as citizens should be to preserve and improve the free society we have inherited.

Problem solving

What are the responsibilities of citizens?

Discuss what responsibilities are implied by the following quotations.

Our public men have, besides politics, their private affairs to attend to, and our ordinary citizens, though occupied with the pursuits of industry, are still fair judges of public matters; for, unlike any other nation, [we Athenians regard] him who takes no part in these duties not as unambitious but as useless...(Pericles' Funeral Oration, 5th century, B.C.)

I may detest what you say, but will defend to the death your right to say it. (Voltaire)

Governments, like clocks, go from the motion men give them; and as governments are made and moved by men, so by them they are ruined, too. Wherefore governments rather depend upon men, than men upon governments. Let men be good, and the government cannot be bad; if it be ill, they will cure it. But, if men be bad, let the government be never so good, they will endeavor to warp and spoil it to their turn. (William Penn, *Frame of Government for Pennsylvania,* 1682.)

If it were to be asked, what is the most sacred duty, and the greatest source of security in a republic, the answer would be, an inviolable respect for the Constitution and the laws--the first growing out of the last. It is by this, in a great degree, that the rich and the powerful are to be restrained from enterprises against the common liberty. (Alexander Hamilton)

It is the manner and spirit of a people which preserve a republic in vigor. (Thomas Jefferson)

. . . I often wonder whether we do not rest our hopes too much upon constitutions, upon laws and upon courts. These are false hopes; believe me, these are false hopes. Liberty lies in the hearts of men and women; when it dies there, no constitution, no law, no court can save it; no constitution, no law, no court can even do much to help it. While it lies there it needs no constitution, no law, no court to save it . . . (Learned Hand, "Liberty," *Yale Alumni Magazine,* June 6, 1941.)

Reviewing and using the lesson

1. Select several rights that American citizens have. For each right you select, state what you believe to be a responsibility that goes with it.

2. If you do not choose to vote or participate in any way in government, should you be required to obey its laws? Why?

3. Should all citizens eligible to vote be required to vote or be subject to a heavy fine? Why?

4. Should a good person obey a bad law? Why?

5. Should a government leave its citizens alone to engage in the "pursuit of happiness" as they see fit? Or should government actively try to raise the standards of its citizens' taste and behavior?

Reference Section

Declaration of Independence

IN CONGRESS,   JULY 4, 1776.

A DECLARATION

BY THE REPRESENTATIVES OF THE

UNITED STATES OF AMERICA,

IN GENERAL CONGRESS ASSEMBLED.

WHEN in the Course of human Events, it becomes necessary for one People to dissolve the Political Bands which have connected them with another, and to assume among the Powers of the Earth, the separate and equal Station to which the Laws of Nature and of Nature's God entitle them, a decent Respect to the Opinions of Mankind requires that they should declare the causes which impel them to the Separation.

We hold these Truths to be self-evident, that all Men are created equal, that they are endowed by their Creator with certain unalienable Rights, that among these are Life, Liberty, and the Pursuit of Happiness-- That to secure these Rights, Governments are instituted among Men, deriving their just Powers from the Consent of the Governed, that whenever any Form of Government becomes destructive of these Ends it is the Right of the People to alter or to abolish it, and to institute new Government, laying its Foundation on such Principles, and organizing its Powers in such Form, as to them shall seem most likely to effect their Safety and Happiness. Prudence, indeed, will dictate that Governments long established should not be changed for light and transient Causes; and accordingly all Experience hath shewn, that Mankind are more disposed to suffer, while Evils are sufferable, than to right themselves by abolishing the Forms to which they are accustomed. But when a long Train of Abuses and Usurpations, pursuing invariably the same Object, evinces a Design to reduce them under absolute Despotism, it is their Right, it is their Duty, to throw off such Government, and to provide new Guards for their future Security. Such has been the patient Sufferance of these Colonies; and such is now the Necessity which constrains them to alter their former Systems of Government. The History of the present King of Great-Britain is a History of repeated Injuries and Usurpations, all having in direct Object the Establishment of an absolute Tyranny over these States. To prove this, let Facts be submitted to a candid World.

He has refused his Assent to Laws, the most wholesome and necessary for the public Good.

He has forbidden his Governors to pass Laws of immediate and pressing Importance, unless suspended in their Operation till his Assent should be obtained; and when so suspended, he has utterly neglected to attend to them.

He has refused to pass other Laws for the Accommodation of large Districts of People, unless those People would relinquish the Right of Representation in the Legislature, a Right inestimable to them, and formidable to Tyrants only.

He has called together Legislative Bodies at Places unusual, uncomfortable, and distant from the Depository of their public Records, for the sole Purpose of fatiguing them into Compliance with his Measures.

He has dissolved Representative Houses repeatedly, for opposing with manly Firmness his Invasions on the Rights of the People.

He has refused for a long Time, after such Dissolutions, to cause others to be elected; whereby the Legislative Powers, incapable of Annihilation, have returned to the People at large for their exercise; the State remaining in the mean time exposed to all the Dangers of Invasions from without, and Convulsions within.

He has endeavored to prevent the Population of these States; for that Purpose obstructing the Laws for Naturalization of Foreigners; refusing to pass others to encourage their Migrations hither, and raising the Conditions of new Appropriations of Lands.

He has obstructed the Administration of Justice, by refusing his Assent to Laws for establishing Judiciary Powers.

He has made Judges dependent on his Will alone, for the Tenure of their Offices, and the Amount and Payment of their Salaries.

He has erected a Multitude of new Offices, and sent hither Swarms of Officers to harass our People and eat out their Substance.

He has kept among us, in Times of Peace, Standing Armies, without the consent of our Legislatures.

He has affected to render the Military independent of and superior to the Civil Power.

He has combined with others to subject us to a Jurisdiction foreign to our Constitution, and unacknowledged by our Laws; giving his Assent to their Acts of pretended Legislation:

For quartering large Bodies of Armed Troops among us:

For protecting them, by a mock Trial, from Punishment for any Murders which they should commit on the Inhabitants of these States:

For cutting off our Trade with all Parts of the World:

For imposing Taxes on us without our Consent:

For depriving us, in many Cases, of the Benefits of Trial by Jury:

For transporting us beyond Seas to be tried for pretended Offenses:

For abolishing the free System of English Laws in a neighbouring Province, establishing therein an Arbitrary Government, and enlarging its Boundaries, so as to render it at once an Example and fit Instrument for introducing the same absolute Rule into these Colonies:

For taking away our Charters, abolishing our most valuable Laws, and altering fundamentally the Forms of our Governments:

For suspending our own Legislatures, and declaring themselves invested with Power to legislate for us in all Cases whatsoever.

He has abdicated Government here, by declaring us out of his Protection and waging War against us.

He has plundered our Seas, ravaged our Coasts, burnt our Towns, and destroyed the Lives of our People.

He is, at this Time, transporting large Armies of foreign Mercenaries to compleat the Works of Death, Desolation, and Tyranny, already begun with circumstances of Cruelty and Perfidy, scarcely paralleled in the most barbarous Ages, and totally unworthy the Head of a civilized Nation.

He has constrained our fellow Citizens taken Captive on the high Seas to bear Arms against their Country, to become the Executioners of their Friends and Brethren, or to fall themselves by their Hands.

He has excited domestic Insurrections amongst us, and has endeavoured to bring on the Inhabitants of our Frontiers, the merciless Indian Savages, whose known Rule of Warfare, is an undistinguished Destruction, of all Ages, Sexes and Conditions.

In every stage of these Oppressions we have Petitioned for Redress in the most humble Terms: Our repeated Petitions have been answered only by repeated Injury. A Prince, whose Character is thus marked by every act which may define a Tyrant, is unfit to be the Ruler of a free People.

Nor have we been wanting in Attentions to our British Brethren. We have warned them from Time to Time of Attempts by their Legislature to extend an unwarrantable Jurisdiction over us. We have reminded them of the Circumstances of our Emigration and Settlement here. We have appealed to their native Justice and Magnanimity, and we have conjured them by the Ties of our common Kindred to disavow these Usurpations, which, would inevitably interrupt our Connections and Correspondence. They too have been deaf to the Voice of Justice and of Consanguinity. We must, therefore, acquiesce in the Necessity, which denounces our Separation, and hold them, as we hold the rest of Mankind, Enemies in War, in Peace, Friends.

We, therefore, the Representatives of the UNITED STATES OF AMERICA, in GENERAL CONGRESS, Assembled, appealing to the Supreme Judge of the World for the Rectitude of our Intentions, do, in the Name, and by Authority of the good People of these Colonies, solemnly Publish and Declare, That these United Colonies are, and of Right ought to be, FREE AND INDEPENDENT STATES; that they are absolved from all Allegiance to the British Crown, and that all political Connection between them and the State of Great-Britain, is and ought to be totally dissolved; and that as FREE AND INDEPENDENT STATES, they have full Power to levy War, conclude Peace, contract Alliances, establish Commerce, and to do all other Acts and Things which INDEPENDENT STATES may of right do. And for the support of this Declaration, with a firm Reliance on the Protection of divine Providence, we mutually pledge to each other our Lives, our Fortunes, and our sacred Honor.

Signed by ORDER and in BEHALF of the CONGRESS,

JOHN HANCOCK, PRESIDENT.

Signers of the Declaration of Independence

New-Hampshire
Josiah Bartlett,
Wm. Whipple,
Matthew Thornton.

Massachusetts-Bay.
Saml. Adams,
John Adams,
Robt. Treat Paine,
Elbridge Gerry.

Rhode-Island and Providence, &c.
Step. Hopkins,
William Ellery.

Connecticut.
Roger Sherman,
Saml. Huntington,
Wm. Williams,
Oliver Wolcott.

New-York
Wm. Floyd,
Phil. Livingston,
Frans. Lewis,
Lewis Morris.

New-Jersey
Richd. Stockton,
Jno. Witherspoon,
Fras. Hopkinson,
John Hart,
Abra. Clark.

Pennsylvania
Robt. Morris,
Benjamin Rush,
Benja. Franklin,
John Morton,
Geo. Clymer,
Jas. Smith
Geo. Taylor,
James Wilson,
Geo. Ross.

Delaware
Casar Rodney,
Geo. Read,
(Tho M:Kean.)

Maryland
Samuel Chase,
Wm. Paca,
Thos. Stone,
Charles Carroll, of Carrollton.

Virginia
George Wythe,
Richard Henry Lee,
Ths. Jefferson,
Benja. Harrison,
Thos. Nelson, jr.
Francis Lightfoot Lee,
Carter Braxton.

North-Carolina.
Wm. Hooper
Joseph Hewes,
John Penn.

South-Carolina.
Edward Rutledge,
Thos. Heyward, junr.
Thomas Lynch, junr.
Arthur Middleton.

Georgia.
Button Gwinnett,
Lyman Hall,
Geo. Walton.

According to the authenticated list printed by order of Congress of January 18, 1777.
Braces, spelling, and abbreviations of names conform to original printed list.

The Constitution of the United States of America

PREAMBLE

We the people of the United States, in order to form a more perfect Union, establish justice, insure domestic tranquility, provide for the common defense, promote the general welfare, and secure the blessings of liberty to ourselves and our posterity, do ordain and establish this Constitution for the United States of America.

ARTICLE I

Section One

All legislative powers herein granted shall be vested in a Congress of the United States, which shall consist of a Senate and House of Representatives.

Section Two

1. The House of Representatives shall be composed of members chosen every second year by the people of the several states, and the electors in each state shall have the qualifications requisite for electors of the most numerous branch of the state legislature.

2. No person shall be a Representative who shall not have attained to the age of twenty-five years, and been seven years a citizen of the United States, and who shall not, when elected, be an inhabitant of that state in which he shall be chosen.

3. [Representatives and direct taxes shall be apporioned among the several states which may be included within this Union, according to their respective numbers, which shall be determined by adding to the whole number of free persons, including those bound to service for a term of years, and excluding Indians not taxed, three fifths of all other persons.]* The actual enumeration shall be made within three years after the first meeting of the Congress of the United States, and within every subsequent term of ten years, in such manner as they shall by law direct. The number of Representatives shall not exceed one for every thirty thousand, but each state shall have at least one Representative; and until such enumeration shall be made, the state of New Hampshire shall be entitled to choose three, Massachusetts eight, Rhode Island and Providence Plantations one, Connecticut five, New York six, New Jersey four, Pennsylvania eight, Delaware one, Maryland six, Virginia ten, North Carolina five, South Carolina five, and Georgia three.

4. When vacancies happen in the representation from any state, the executive authority thereof shall issue writs of election to fill such vacancies.

5. The House of Representatives shall choose their speaker and other officers; and shall have the sole power of impeachment.

Section Three

1. [The Senate of the United States shall be composed of two Senators from each state, chosen by the legislature thereof, for six years; and each Senator shall have one vote.]

2. Immediately after they shall be assembled in consequence of the first election, they shall be divided as equally as may be into three classes. The seats of the Senators of the first class shall be vacated at the expiration of the second year, of the second class at the expiration of the fourth year, and of the third class at the expiration of the sixth year, so that one third may be chosen every second year; and if vacancies happen by resignation, or otherwise, during the recess of the legislature of any state, the executive thereof may make temporary appointments [until the next meeting of the legislature, which shall then fill such vacancies.]

3. No person shall be a Senator who shall not have attained to the age of thirty years, and been nine years a citizen of the United States, and who shall not, when elected, be an inhabitant of that state for which he shall be chosen.

4. The Vice-President of the United States shall be president of the Senate, but shall have no vote unless they be equally divided.

5. The Senate shall choose their other officers, and also a president pro tempore, in the absence of the Vice-President, or when he shall exercise the office of President of the United States.

6. The Senate shall have the sole power to try all impeachments. When sitting for that purpose, they shall be on oath or affirmation. When the President of the United States is tried, the Chief Justice shall

---

*This is the original text. Passages in brackets indicate that they were affected by Amendments.

preside; and no person shall be convicted without the concurrence of two-thirds of the members present.

7. Judgment in cases of impeachment shall not extend further than to removal from office, and disqualification to hold and enjoy any office of honor, trust, or profit under the United States; but the party convicted shall nevertheless be liable and subject to indictment, trial, judgment, and punishment, according to law.

Section Four

1. The times, places, and manner of holding elections for Senators and Representatives shall be prescribed in each state by the legislature thereof, but the Congress may at any time by law make or alter such regulations except as to the place of choosing Senators.

2. [The Congress shall assemble at least once in every year, and such meeting shall be on the first Monday in December, unless they shall by law appoint a different day.]

Section Five

1. Each House shall be the judge of the elections, returns, and qualifications of its own members, and a majority of each shall constitute a quorum to do business; but a smaller number may adjourn from day to day, and may be authorized to compel the attendance of absent members, in such manner, and under such penalties as each House may provide.

2. Each House may determine the rules of its proceedings, punish its members for disorderly behavior, and, with the concurrence of two-thirds, expel a member.

3. Each House shall keep a journal of its proceedings, and from time to time publish the same, excepting such parts as may in their judgment require secrecy; and the yeas and nays of the members of either House on any question shall, at the desire of one-fifth of those present, be entered on the journal.

4. Neither House, during the session of Congress, shall, without the consent of the other, adjourn for more than three days, nor to any other place than that in which the two Houses shall be sitting.

Section Six

1. The Senators and Representatives shall receive a compensation for their services, to be ascertained by law, and paid out of the Treasury of the United States. They shall in all cases, except treason, felony and breach of the peace, be privileged from arrest during their attendance at the session of their respective Houses, and in going to and returning from the same; and for any speech or debate in either House, they shall not be questioned in any other place.

2. No Senator or Representative shall, during the time for which he was elected, be appointed to any civil office under the authority of the United States, which shall have been created, or the emoluments whereof shall have been increased during such time; and no person holding any office under the United States shall be a member of either House during his continuance in office.

Section Seven

1. All bills for raising revenue shall originate in the House of Representatives; but the Senate may propose or concur with amendments as on other bills.

2. Every bill which shall have passed the House of Representatives and the Senate, shall, before it become a law, be presented to the President of the United States; if he approve he shall sign it, but if not he shall return it, with his objections, to that House in which it shall have originated, who shall enter the objections at large on their journal, and proceed to reconsider it. If after such reconsideration two-thirds of that House shall agree to pass the bill, it shall be sent, together with the objections, to the other House, by which it shall likewise be reconsidered, and if approved by two-thirds of that House, it shall become a law. But in all such cases the votes of both Houses shall be determined by yeas and nays, and the names of the persons voting for and against the bill shall be entered on the journal of each House respectively. If any bill shall not be returned by the President within ten days (Sundays excepted) after it shall have been presented to him, the same shall be a law, in like manner as if he had signed it, unless the Congress by their adjournment prevent its return, in which case it shall not be a law.

3. Every order, resolution, or vote to which the concurrence of the Senate and House of Representatives may be necessary (except on a question of adjournment) shall be presented to the President of the

United States; and before the same shall take effect, shall be approved by him, or being disapproved by him, shall be repassed by two-thirds of the Senate and House of Representatives, according to the rules and limitations prescribed in the case of a bill.

Section Eight

The Congress shall have power:

1. To lay and collect taxes, duties, imposts and excises, to pay the debts and provide for the common defense and general welfare of the United States; but all duties, imposts and excises shall be uniform throughout the United States;

2. To borrow money on the credit of the United States;

3. To regulate commerce with foreign nations, and among the several States, and with the Indian tribes;

4. To establish an uniform rule of naturalization, and uniform laws on the subject of bankruptcies throughout the United States;

5. To coin money, regulate the value thereof, and of foreign coin, and fix the standard of weights and measures;

6. To provide for the punishment of counterfeiting the securities and current coin of the United States;

7. To establish post offices and post roads;

8. To promote the progress of science and useful arts, by securing for limited time to authors and inventors the exclusive right to their respective writings and discoveries;

9. To constitute tribunals inferior to the Supreme Court;

10. To define and punish piracies and felonies committed on the high seas, and offenses against the law of nations;

11. To declare war, grant letters of marque and reprisal, and make rules concerning captures on land and water;

12. To raise and support armies, but no appropriation of money to that use shall be for a longer term than two years;

13. To provide and maintain a navy;

14. To make rules for the government and regulation of the land and naval forces;

15. To provide for calling forth the militia to execute the laws of the Union, suppress insurrections and repel invasions;

16. To provide for organizing, arming and disciplining the militia, and for governing such part of them as may be employed in the service of the United States, reserving to the states respectively, the appointment of the officers, and the authority of training the militia according to the discipline prescribed by Congress;

17. To exercise exclusive legislation in all cases whatsoever, over such district (not exceeding ten miles square) as may, by session of particular states, and the acceptance of Congress, become the seat of the government of the United States, and to exercise like authority over all places purchased by the consent of the legislature of the state in which the same shall be, for the erection of forts, magazines, arsenals, dockyards, and other needful buildings; - and

18. To make all laws which shall be necessary and proper for carrying into execution the foregoing powers, and all other powers vested by this Constitution in the Government of the United States, or in any department or officer thereof.

Section Nine

1. The migration or importation of such persons as any of the states now existing shall think proper to admit, shall not be prohibited by the Congress prior to the year one thousand eight hundred and eight, but a tax or duty may be imposed on such importation, not exceeding ten dollars for each person.

2. The privilege of the writ of habeas corpus shall not be suspended, unless when in cases of rebellion or invasion the public safety may require it.

3. No bill of attainder or ex post facto law shall be passed.

4. No capitation, or other direct, tax shall be laid, unless in proportion to the census or enumeration herein before directed to be taken.

5. No tax or duty shall be laid on articles exported from any state.

6. No preference shall be given by any regulation of commerce or revenue to the ports of one state over those of another; nor shall vessels bound to, or from,

one state, be obliged to enter clear, or pay duties in another.

7. No money shall be drawn from the treasury but in consequence of appropriations made by law; and a regular statement and account of the receipts and expenditures of all public money shall be published from time to time.

8. No title of nobility shall be granted by the United States: And no person holding any office of profit or trust under them, shall, without the consent of the Congress, accept of any present, emolument, office, or title, of any kind whatever from any king, prince, or foreign state.

Section Ten

1. No state shall enter into any treaty, alliance, or confederation; grant letters of marque and reprisal; coin money; emit bills of credit; make any thing but gold and silver coin a tender in payment of debts; pass any bill of attainder, ex post facto law, or law impairing the obligation of contracts, or grant any title of nobility.

2. No state shall, without the consent of the Congress, lay any imposts or duties on imports or exports, except what may be absolutely necessary for executing its inspection laws; and the net produce of all duties and imposts, laid by any state on imports or exports, shall be for the use of the treasury of the United States; and all such laws shall be subject to the revision and control of the Congress.

3. No state shall, without the consent of Congress, lay any duty of tonnage, keep troops, or ships of war in time of peace, enter into any agreement or compact with another state or with a foreign power, or engage in war, unless actually invaded, or in such imminent danger as will not admit of delay.

ARTICLE II

Section One

1. The executive power shall be vested in a President of the United States of America. He shall hold his office during the term of four years, and, together with the Vice-President, chosen for the same term, be elected, as follows:

2. Each state shall appoint, in such manner as the legislature therefore may direct, a number of electors, equal to the whole number of Senators and Representatives to which the state may be entitled in the Con-

gress; but no Senator or Representative, or person holding an office of trust or profit under the United States, shall be appointed an elector.

3. [The Electors shall meet in their respective states, and vote by ballot for two persons, of whom one at least shall not be an inhabitant of the same state with themselves. And they shall make a list of all the persons voted for, and of the number of votes for each; which list they shall sign and certify, and transmit sealed to the seat of the Government of the United States, directed to the President of the Senate. The President of the Senate shall, in the presence of the Senate and House of Representatives, open all the certificates, and the votes shall then be counted. The person having the greatest number of votes shall be the President, if such number be a majority of the whole number of electors appointed; and if there be more than one who have such majority, and have an equal number of votes, then the House of Representatives shall immediately choose by ballot one of them for President; and if no person have a majority, then from the five highest on the list the said House shall in like manner choose the President. But in choosing the President, the votes shall be taken by states, the representation from each state having one vote; a quorum for this purpose shall consist of a member or members from two-thirds of the states, and a majority of all the states shall be necessary to a choice. In every case, after the choice of the President, the person having the greatest number of votes of the electors shall be the Vice-President. But if there should remain two or more who have equal votes, the Senate shall choose from them by ballot the Vice-President.]

4. The Congress may determine the time of choosing the electors, and the day on which they shall give their votes; which day shall be the same throughout the United States.

5. No person except a natural born citizen, or a citizen of the United States, at the time of the adoption of this Constitution, shall be eligible to the office of President; neither shall any person be eligible to that office who shall not have attained to the age of thirty-five years, and been fourteen years a resident within the United States.

6. [In case of the removal of the President from office, or of his death, resignation, or inability to discharge the powers and duties of the said office, the same shall devolve on the Vice-President, and the Congress may by law provide for the case of removal, death, resignation or inability, both of the President and Vice-President, declaring what officer shall then act as President, and such officer shall act according-

ly, until the disability be removed, or a President shall be elected.]

7. The President shall, at stated times, receive for his services, a compensation, which shall neither be increased nor diminished during the period for which he shall have been elected, and he shall not receive within that period any other emolument from the United States, or any of them.

8. Before he enter the execution of this office, he shall take the following oath or affirmation:

"I do solemnly swear (or affirm) that I will faithfully execute the office of President of the United States, and will to the best of my ability, preserve, protect and defend the Constitution of the United States."

Section Two

1. The President shall be Commander in Chief of the army and navy of the United States, and of the militia of the several states, when called into the actual service of the United States; he may require the opinion, in writing, of the principal officer in each of the executive departments, upon any subject relating to the duties of their respective offices, and he shall have power to grant reprieves and pardons for offenses against the United States, except in cases of impeachment.

2. He shall have power, by and with the advice and consent of the Senate, to make treaties, provided two-thirds of the Senators present concur; and he shall nominate, and by and with the advice and consent of the Senate, shall appoint ambassadors, other public ministers and consuls, judges of the Supreme Court, and all other officers of the United States, whose appointments are not herein otherwise provided for, and which shall be established by law; but the Congress may by law vest the appointment of such inferior officers, as they think proper, in the President alone, in the courts of law, or in the heads of departments.

3. The President shall have power to fill up all vacancies that may happen during the recess of the Senate, by granting commissions which shall expire at the end of their next session.

Section Three

He shall from time to time give to the Congress information of the state of the Union, and recommend to their consideration such measures as he shall judge necessary and expedient; he may, on extraordinary occasions, convene both Houses, or either of them, and in case of disagreement between them, with respect to the time of adjournment, he may adjourn them to such time as he shall think proper; he shall receive ambassadors and other public ministers; he shall take care that the laws be faithfully executed, and shall commission all the officers of the United States.

Section Four

The President, Vice-President and all civil officers of the United States, shall be removed from office on impeachment for, and conviction of, treason, bribery, or other high crimes and misdemeanors.

ARTICLE III

Section One

The judicial power of the United States, shall be vested in one Supreme Court, and in such inferior courts as the Congress may from time to time ordain and establish. The judges, both of the Supreme and inferior courts, shall hold their offices during good behavior, and shall, at stated times, receive for their services a compensation, which shall not be diminished during their continuance in office.

Section Two

1. The judicial power shall extend to all cases, in law and equity, arising under this Constitution, the laws of the United States, and treaties made, or which shall be made, under their authority; to all cases affecting ambassadors, other public ministers and consuls; to all cases of admiralty and maritime jurisdiction; to controversies to which the United States shall be a party; to controversies between two or more states; between a state and citizens of another state; between citizens of different states; between citizens of the same state claiming lands under grants of different states, and [between a state, or the citizens thereof, and foreign states, citizens or subjects.]

2. In all cases affecting ambassadors, other public ministers and consuls, and those in which a state shall be party, the Supreme Court shall have original jurisdiction. In all the other cases before mentioned, the Supreme Court shall have appellate jurisdiction, both as to law and fact, with such exceptions, and under such regulations as the Congress shall make.

3. The trial of all crimes, except in cases of impeachment, shall be by jury; and such trial shall be held in the state where said crimes shall have been committed; but when not committed within any state, the

trial shall be at such place or places as the Congress may by law have directed.

Section Three

1. Treason against the United States, shall consist only in levying war against them, or in adhering to their enemies, giving them aid and comfort. No person shall be convicted of treason unless on the testimony of two witnesses to the same overt act, or on confession in open court.

2. The Congress shall have power to declare the punishment of treason, but no attainder of treason shall work corruption of blood or forfeiture except during the life of the person attainted.

ARTICLE IV

Section One

Full faith and credit shall be given in each state to the public acts, records, and judicial proceedings of every other state. And the Congress may by general laws prescribe the manner in which such acts, records and proceedings shall be proved, and the effect thereof.

Section Two

1. The citizens of each state shall be entitled to all privileges and immunities of citizens in the several states.

2. A person charged in any state with treason, felony, or other crime, who shall flee from justice, and be found in another state, shall on demand of the executive authority of the state, from which he fled, be delivered up, to be removed to the state having jurisdiction of the crime.

3. [No person held to service or labor in one state, under the laws thereof, escaping into another, shall, in consequence of any law or regulation therein, be discharged from such service or labor, but shall be delivered up on claim of the party to whom such service or labor may be due.]

Section Three

1. New states may be admitted by the Congress into this Union, but no new state shall be formed or erected within the jurisdiction of any other state; nor any state be formed by the junction of two or more states, or parts of states, without the consent of the

legislatures of the states concerned as well as of the Congress.

2. The Congress shall have power to dispose of and make all needful rules and regulations respecting the territory or other property belonging to the United States, and nothing in this Constitution shall be so construed as to prejudice any claims of the United States, or of any particular state.

Section Four

The United States shall guarantee to every state in this Union a republican form of government, and shall protect each of them against invasion; and on application of the legislature, or of the executive (when the legislature cannot be convened) against domestic violence.

ARTICLE V

The Congress, whenever two-thirds of both Houses shall deem it necessary, shall propose amendments to this Constitution, or, on the application of the legislatures of two-thirds of the several states, shall call a convention for proposing amendments, which, in either case, shall be valid to all intents and purposes, as part of this Constitution, when ratified by the legislatures of three-fourths of the several states, or by conventions in three-fourths thereof, as the one or the other mode of ratification may be proposed by the Congress; provided that no amendment which may be made prior to the year one thousand eight hundred and eight shall in any manner affect the first and fourth clauses in the ninth section of the first article; and that no state, without its consent, shall be deprived of its equal suffrage in the Senate.

ARTICLE VI

1. All debts contracted and engagements entered into, before the adoption of this Constitution, shall be as valid against the United States under this Constitution, as under the confederation.

2. This Constitution, and the laws of the United States which shall be made in pursuance thereof; and all treaties made, or which shall be made, under the authority of the United States, shall be the supreme law of the land; and the judges in every state shall be bound thereby, anything in the Constitution or laws of any state to the contrary notwithstanding.

3. The Senators and Representatives before mentioned, and the members of the several state legisla-

tures, and all executive and judicial officers, both of the United States and of the several states, shall be bound by oath or affirmation, to support this Constitution; but no religious test shall ever be required as a qualification to any office or public trust under the United States.

ARTICLE VII

The ratification of the conventions of nine states, shall be sufficient for the establishment of this Constitution between the states so ratifying the same.

Done in Convention, by the unanimous consent of the States present, the seventeenth day of September, in the year of our Lord one thousand seven hundred and eighty-seven, and of the independence of the United States of America the twelfth. In witness whereof we have hereunto subscribed our names.

George Washington, President,
and Deputy from Virginia.

(This Constitution was adopted on September 17, 1787 by the Constitutional Convention, and was declared ratified on July 2, 1788.)

Signers of the Constitution

New Hampshire
John Langdon
Nicholas Gilman

Massachusetts
Nathaniel Gorham
Rufus King

Connecticut
William Samuel Johnson
Roger Sherman

New York
Alexander Hamilton

New Jersey
William Livingston
David Brearley
William Paterson
Jonathan Dayton

Pennsylvania
Benjamin Franklin
Thomas Mifflin
Robert Morris
George Clymer
Thomas Fitzsimons
Jared Ingersoll
James Wilson
Gouverneur Morris

Delaware
George Read
Gunning Bedford, Jr.
John Dickinson
Richard Bassett
Jacob Broom

Maryland
James McHenry
Daniel of St. Tho. Jenifer
Daniel Carrol

Virginia
John Blair
James Madison, Junior.

North Carolina
William Blount
Richard Dobbs Spaight
Hugh Williamson

South Carolina
John Rutledge
Charles Cotesworth Pinckney
Charles Pinckney
Pierce Butler

Georgia
William Few
Abraham Baldwin

Attest: William Jackson,
Secretary

AMENDMENTS TO THE CONSTITUTION

Since 1787, twenty-six amendments have been proposed by the Congress and ratified by the several states, pursuant to the fifth Article of the original Constitution.

Amendment I

Congress shall make no law respecting an establishment of religion, or prohibiting the free exercise thereof; or abridging the freedom of speech, or of the press; or the right of the people peaceably to assemble, and to petition the Government for a redress of grievances. (Ratified December, 1791.)

Amendment II

A well regulated Militia, being necessary to the security of a free State, the right of the people to keep and bear Arms, shall not be infringed. (Ratified December, 1791.)

Amendment III

No Soldier shall, in time of peace be quartered in any house without the consent of the Owner, nor in time of war, but in a manner to be prescribed by law. (Ratified December, 1791.)

Amendment IV

The right of the people to be secure in their persons, houses, papers, and effects, against unreasonable searches and seizures, shall not be violated, and no Warrants shall issue, but upon probable cause, supported by Oath or affirmation, and particularly describing the place to be searched, and the persons or things to be seized. (Ratified December, 1791.)

Amendment V

No person shall be held to answer for a capital, or otherwise infamous crime, unless on a presentment or indictment of a Grand Jury, except in cases arising in the land or naval forces, or in the Militia, when in actual service in time of War or public danger; nor shall any person be subject for the same offence to be twice put in jeopardy of life or limb; nor shall be compelled in any criminal case to be a witness against himself, nor be deprived of life, liberty, or property, without due process of law; nor shall private property be taken for public use, without just compensation. (Ratified December, 1791.)

Amendment VI

In all criminal prosecutions, the accused shall enjoy the right to a speedy and public trial, by an impartial jury of the State and district wherein the crime shall have been committed, which district shall have been previously ascertained by law, and to be informed of the nature and cause of the accusation; to be confronted with the witnesses against him; to have compulsory process for obtaining witnesses in his favor, and to have the assistance of counsel for his defence. (Ratified December, 1791.)

Amendment VII

In Suits at common law, where the value in controversy shall exceed twenty dollars, the right of trial by jury shall be preserved, and no fact tried by a jury, shall be otherwise re-examined in any Court of the United States, than according to the rules of the common law. (Ratified December, 1791.)

Amendment VIII

Excessive bail shall not be required, nor excessive fines imposed, nor cruel and unusual punishments inflicted. (Ratified December, 1791.)

Amendment IX

The enumeration in the Constitution, of certain rights, shall not be construed to deny or disparage others retained by the people. (Ratified December, 1791.)

Amendment X

The powers not delegated to the United States by the Constitution, nor prohibited by it to the States, are reserved to the States respectively, or to the people. (Ratified December, 1791.)

Amendment XI

The Judicial power of the United States shall not be construed to extend to any suit in law or equity, commenced or prosecuted against one of the United States by Citizens of another State, or by Citizens or Subjects of any Foreign State. (Ratified February, 1795.)

Amendment XII

The Electors shall meet in their respective states, and vote by ballot for President and Vice-President, one of whom, at least, shall not be an inhabitant of the same state with themselves; they shall name in their ballots the person voted for as President, and in distinct ballots the person voted for as Vice-President, and they shall make distinct lists of all persons voted for as President, and of all persons voted for as Vice-President, and of the number of votes for each, which lists they shall sign and certify, and transmit sealed to the seat of the government of the United States, directed to the President of the Senate;--The President of the Senate shall, in the presence of the Senate and House of Representatives, open all the certificates and the votes shall then be counted;--The person having the greatest number of votes for President, shall be the President, if such number be a majority of the whole number of Electors appointed; and if no person have such majority, then from the persons having the highest numbers not exceeding three on the list of those voted for as President, the House of Representatives shall choose immediately, by ballot, the President. But in choosing the President, the votes shall be taken by states, the representation from each state having one vote; a quorum for this purpose shall consist of a member or members from two-thirds of the states, and a majority of all the states shall be necessary to a choice. [And if the House of Representatives shall not choose a President whenever the right of choice shall devolve upon them, before the fourth day of March next following, then the Vice-President shall act as President, as in the case of the death or other constitutional disability of the President.] The person having the greatest number of votes as Vice-President, shall be the Vice-President, if such number be a majority of the whole number of Electors appointed, and if no person have a majority, then from the two highest numbers on the list, the Senate shall choose the Vice-President; a quorum for the purpose shall consist of two-thirds of the whole number of Senators, and a majority of the whole number shall be necessary to a choice. But no person constitutionally ineligible to the office of President shall be eligible to that of Vice-President of the United States. (Ratified June, 1804.)

Amendment XIII

Section 1. Neither slavery nor involuntary servitude, except as a punishment for crime whereof the party shall have been duly convicted, shall exist within the United States, or any place subject to their jurisdiction.

Section 2. Congress shall have power to enforce this article by appropriate legislation. (Ratified December, 1865.)

Amendment XIV

Section 1. All persons born or naturalized in the United States, and subject to the jurisdiction thereof, are citizens of the United States and of the State wherein they reside. No State shall make or enforce any law which shall abridge the privileges or immunities of citizens of the United States; nor shall any State deprive any person of life, liberty, or property, without due process of law; nor deny to any person within its jurisdiction the equal protection of the laws.

Section 2. Representatives shall be apportioned among the several States according to their respective numbers, counting the whole number of persons in each State, excluding Indians not taxed. But when the right to vote at any election for the choice of electors for President and Vice President of the United States,

Representatives in Congress, the Executive and Judicial officers of a State, or the members of the Legislature thereof, is denied to any of the male inhabitants of such State, being twenty-one years of age, and citizens of the United States, or in any way abridged, except for participation in rebellion, or other crime, the basis of representation therein shall be reduced in the proportion which the number of such male citizens shall bear to the whole number of male citizens twenty-one years of age in such State.

Section 3. No person shall be a Senator or a Representative in Congress, or elector of President and Vice-President, or hold any office, civil or military, under the United States, or under any State, who, having previously taken an oath, as a member of Congress, or as an officer of the United States, or as a member of any State legislature, or as an executive or judicial officer of any State, to support the Constitution of the United States, shall have engaged in insurrection or rebellion against the same, or given aid or comfort to the enemies thereof. But Congress may by a vote of two-thirds of each House, remove such disability.

Section 4. The validity of the public debt of the United States, authorized by law, including debts incurred for payment of pensions and bounties for services in suppressing insurrection or rebellion, shall not be questioned. But neither the United States nor any State shall assume or pay any debt or obligation incurred in aid of insurrection or rebellion against the United States, or any claim for the loss or emancipation of any slave; but all such debts, obligations and claims shall be held illegal and void.

Section 5. The Congress shall have power to enforce, by appropriate legislation, the provisions of this article. (Ratified July, 1868.)

Amendment XV

Section 1. The right of citizens of the United States to vote shall not be denied or abridged by the United States or by any State on account of race, color, or previous condition of servitude.

Section 2. The Congress shall have power to enforce this article by appropriate legislation. (Ratified February, 1870.)

Amendment XVI

The Congress shall have power to lay and collect taxes on incomes, from whatever source derived, without apportionment among the several States, and without regard to any census or enumeration. (Ratified February, 1913.)

Amendment XVII

The Senate of the United States shall be composed of two Senators from each State, elected by the people thereof, for six years; and each Senator shall have one vote. The electors in each State shall have the qualifications requisite for electors of the most numerous branch of the State legislatures.

When vacancies happen in the representation of any State in the Senate, the executive authority of such State shall issue writs of election to fill such vacancies: *Provided,* That the legislature of any State may empower the executive thereof to make temporary appointments until the people fill the vacancies by election as the legislature may direct.

This amendment shall not be so construed as to affect the election or term of any Senator chosen before it becomes valid as part of the Constitution. (Ratified April, 1913.)

Amendment XVIII

[Section 1. After one year from the ratification of this article the manufacture, sale, or transportation of intoxicating liquors within, the importation thereof into, or the exportation thereof from the United States and all territory subject to the jurisdiction thereof for beverage purposes is hereby prohibited.

Section 2. The Congress and Several States shall have concurrent power to enforce this article by appropriate legislation.

Section 3. This article shall be inoperative unless it shall have been ratified as an amendment to the Constitution by the legislatures of the several States, as provided in the Constitution, within seven years from the date of the submission hereof to the States by the Congress.] (Ratified January, 1919.)

Amendment XIX

The right of citizens of the United States to vote shall not be denied or abridged by the United States or by any State on account of sex.

Congress shall have power to enforce this article by appropriate legislation. (Ratified August, 1920.)

Amendment XX

Section 1. The terms of the President and Vice President shall end at noon on the 20th day of January, and the terms of Senators and Representatives at noon on the 3d day of January, of the years in which such terms would have ended if this article had not been ratified; and the terms of their successors shall then begin.

Section 2. The Congress shall assemble at least once in every year, and such meeting shall begin at noon on the 3d day of January, unless they shall by law appoint a different day.

Section 3. If, at the time fixed for the beginning of the term of the President, the President elect shall have died, the Vice President elect shall become President. If a President shall not have been chosen before the time fixed for the beginning of his term, or if the President elect shall have failed to qualify, then the Vice President elect shall act as President until a President shall have qualified; and the Congress may by law provide for the case wherein neither a President elect nor a Vice President elect shall have qualified, declaring who shall then act as President, or the manner in which one who is to act shall be selected, and such person shall act accordingly until a President or Vice President shall have qualified.

Section 4. The Congress may by law provide for the case of the death of any of the persons from whom the House of Representatives may choose a President whenever the right of choice shall have devolved upon them, and for the case of the death of any of the persons from whom the Senate may choose a Vice President whenever the right of choice shall have devolved upon them.

Section 5. Sections 1 and 2 shall take effect on the 15th day of October following the ratification of this article.

Section 6. This article shall be inoperative unless it shall have been ratified as an amendment to the Constitution by the legislatures of three-fourths of the several States within seven years from the date of its submission. (Ratified January, 1933.)

Amendment XXI

Section 1. The eighteenth article of amendment to the Constitution of the United States is hereby repealed.

Section 2. The transportation or importation into any State, Territory, or possession of the United States for delivery or use therein of intoxicating liquors, in violation of the laws thereof, is hereby prohibited.

Section 3. This article shall be inoperative unless it shall have been ratified as an amendment to the Constitution by conventions in the several States, as provided in the Constitution, within seven years from the date of the submission hereof to the States by the Congress. (Ratified December, 1933.)

Amendment XXII

Section 1. No person shall be elected to the office of the President more than twice, and no person who has held the office of President, or acted as President, for more than two years of a term to which some other person was elected President shall be elected to the office of the President more than once. But this Article shall not apply to any person holding the office of President when this Article was proposed by the Congress, and shall not prevent any person who may be holding the office of President, or acting as President, during the term within which this Article becomes operative from holding the office of President or acting as President during the remainder of such term.

Section 2. This article shall be inoperative unless it shall have been ratified as an amendment to the Constitution by the legislatures of three-fourths of the several States within seven years from the date of its submission to the States by the Congress. (Ratified February, 1951.)

Amendment XXIII

Section 1. The District constituting the seat of Government of the United States shall appoint in such manner as the Congress may direct:

A number of electors of President and Vice President equal to the whole number of Senators and Representatives in Congress to which the District would be entitled if it were a State, but in no event more than the least populous State; they shall be in addition to those appointed by the States, but they shall be considered, for the purposes of the election of President and Vice President, to be electors appointed by a State; and they shall meet in the District and perform such duties as provided by the twelfth article of amendment.

Section 2. The Congress shall have power to enforce this article by appropriate legislation. (Ratified March, 1961.)

Amendment XXIV

Section 1. The right of citizens of the United States to vote in any primary or other election for President or Vice President, for electors for President or Vice President, or for Senator or Representative in Congress, shall not be denied or abridged by the United States or any State by reason of failure to pay any poll tax or other tax.

Section 2. The Congress shall have power to enforce this article by appropriate legislation. (Ratified January, 1964.)

Amendment XXV

Section 1. In case of removal of the President from office or of his death or resignation, the Vice President shall become President.

Section 2. Whenever there is a vacancy in the office of the Vice President, the President shall nominate a Vice President who shall take office upon confirmation by a majority vote of both Houses of Congress.

Section 3. Whenever the President transmits to the President pro tempore of the Senate and the Speaker of the House of Representatives his written declaration that he is unable to discharge the powers and duties of his office, and until he transmits to them a written declaration to the contrary, such powers and duties shall be discharged by the Vice President as Acting President.

Section 4. Whenever the Vice President and a majority of either the principal officers of the executive departments or of such other body as Congress may by law provide, transmit to the President pro tempore of the Senate and the Speaker of the House of Representatives their written declaration that the President is unable to discharge the powers and duties of his office, the Vice President shall immediately assume the powers and duties of the office as Acting President.

Thereafter, when the President transmits to the President pro tempore of the Senate and the Speaker of the House of Representatives his written declaration that no inability exists, he shall resume the powers and duties of his office unless the Vice President and a majority of either the principal officers of the executive department or of such other body as Congress may by law provide, transmit within four days to the President pro tempore of the Senate and the Speaker of the House of Representatives their written declaration that the President is unable to discharge the powers and duties of his office. Thereupon Congress shall decide the issue, assembling within forty-eight hours for that purpose if not in session. If the Congress, within twenty-one days after receipt of the latter written declaration, or, if Congress is not in session, within twenty-one days after Congress is required to assemble, determines by two-thirds vote of both Houses that the President is unable to discharge the powers and duties of his office, the Vice President shall continue to discharge the same as Acting President; otherwise, the President shall resume the powers and duties of his office. (Ratified February, 1967.)

Amendment XXVI

Section 1. The right of citizens of the United States, who are eighteen years of age or older, to vote shall not be denied or abridged by the United States or by any State on account of age.

Section 2. The Congress shall have power to enforce this article by appropriate legislation. (Ratified July, 1971.)

Glossary of Major Terms and Concepts

advocacy. The act of speaking or writing in favor or support of something.

affirmative action. A requirement or policy, imposed by law or administrative regulation, that an organization take positive steps to increase the number or proportion of women and minorities in its membership.

alien. Anyone not a citizen of one's own country.

anarchy. Absence of government or laws; a state of political disorder, due to the absence of governmental authority.

Anti-Federalists. The early political leaders who were against the ratification of the Constitution because they thought it gave too much power to the national government and did not protect the political rights of the people.

appellate jurisdiction. The legal authority of a court to hear appeals from a lower court.

aristocracy. A form of government in which power is exercised by a small ruling class, without a monarch and without representation of the common people.

Articles of Confederation. The constitution of the thirteen original American colonies, adopted by Congress in 1781 and replaced in 1788 by the Constitution of the United States.

authority. The right to control or direct the actions of others, in accordance with law, morality, or custom.

autocratic or dictatorial government. A government in which the rulers, whether one or many, exercise unlimited power.

bill of attainder. An act of the legislature that inflicts punishment on a named individual or group without a judicial trial.

Bill of Rights. The first ten amendments to the Constitution which restrict the federal government's power to interfere with certain basic rights of the people.

cabinet. The heads of the departments of the executive branch who advise the president.

checks and balances. The distribution and balancing of power among different branches of government so that no one branch is able to dominate the others.

citizen. A person who is a member of a political society and therefore owes allegiance to and is entitled to protection by and from the government.

civic virtue. The dedication of citizens to the common welfare, even at the cost of their individual interests.

common law. The body of unwritten law developed in England from judicial decisions based on custom and earlier judicial decisions, which constitutes the basis of the English legal system and became part of American law.

common welfare. The good of the community as a whole.

commons. The mass of the people, as distinguished from the nobility. In Great Britain, they are represented in the House of Commons.

confederation. A form of political organization in which the sovereign states combine for certain specified purposes such as defense. The United States was a confederation from 1776 to 1787.

constitution. A set of customs, traditions, rules, and laws that sets forth the way a government is organized and operated.

constitutional democracy. A form of government in which majority rule is limited by a constitution.

constitutional government. A government in which the powers of the ruler or rulers are limited by a constitution which they must obey.

contract. A binding agreement between two or more persons. Each side in a contract agrees to do something in consideration of the other side doing something.

corrupt government. A distorted form of government in which rulers serve their own interests at the expense of the common welfare.

democracy. A form of government in which political control is exercised by all the people, either directly or through their elected representatives.

divine right. The theory of government that holds that a monarch receives the right to rule directly from God and not from the people.

double jeopardy. The provision in the Fifth Amendment that one may not be tried twice for the same crime, "be twice put in jeopardy of life or limb . . ."

electoral college. The group of presidential electors that casts the official votes for president after a presidential election. Each state has a number equal to the total of its members in the Senate and House of Representatives.

England. One of the three countries which make up the island of Great Britain. England was united with Scotland and Wales in 1707 to form Great Britain.

English Bill of Rights. An act passed by Parliament in 1689, which limited the power of the monarch. This document established Parliament as the most powerful branch of the English government.

enumerated powers. Powers that are specifically granted to Congress by Article I, Section 8 of the Constitution.

equal protection clause. The clause in the first section of the 14th Amendment that prohibits states from denying "any person . . . the equal protection of the laws."

ex post facto law. A law that declares an act a crime, even though it was not a crime when committed. Ex post facto laws are forbidden by the Constitution (Article I, Sections 9 and 10).

executive branch. The branch of government that carries out the laws made by the legislative branch; and in the national government, makes treaties with foreign governments and conducts wars.

faction. A group, according to James Madison, that seeks to promote its own special interests at the expense of the common welfare.

federal bureaucracy. The agencies of the executive branch of the federal government.

federal system (or federalism). A form of political organization in which governmental power is divided between a central government and territorial subdivisions--in the United States, among the national, state, and local governments.

Federalist, The. A series of articles written in 1787-1788 by Alexander Hamilton, James Madison, and John Jay, urging the adoption of the Constitution and supporting the need for a strong national government.

Federalists. The people who supported the ratification of the Constitution and advocated a strong central government.

feudalism. A system of government in which a king or queen shared power with the nobility, who required services from the common people in return for allowing them to use the noble's land.

Founders. The people who played important roles in the development of the national government of the United States.

Framers. The delegates to the Philadelphia Convention held in 1787.

general welfare clause. Clause in Article I, Section 8 of the Constitution which gives Congress power to provide for "the general welfare of the United States."

government. The organization through which political control is exercised in a society.

Great Britain. The island consisting of England, Scotland, and Wales. Today, Great Britain is part of the United Kingdom of Great Britain and Northern Ireland.

Great Compromise (Connecticut Compromise). The plan adopted at the Philadelphia Convention in which Congress would be composed of a Senate, with two members from each state; and a House of Representatives, with the members from each state determined by the size of its population.

habeas corpus, writ of. A Latin term meaning, "you shall have the body." It is an order commanding that a prisoner be brought to court to be told why he is being detained.

higher law. As used in describing a legal system, refers to the superiority of one set of laws over another. For example, the Constitution is a higher law than any federal or state law. In the natural rights philosophy, it means that natural law and divine law are superior to laws made by human beings.

House of Commons. One of two houses of the English Parliament; represents the common people.

House of Lords. The one of the two houses of the English Parliament which represents the nobility.

human nature. Those traits, if any, of personality and character that all people have in common.

impeachment. Charging a public official with a crime in office.

implied powers. Powers of Congress to make all laws that are "necessary and proper" for carrying out the powers expressly delegated to it by the Constitution. (Article I, Section 8)

incorporation. The Supreme Court interpretations of the 14th Amendment which have extended the protections of the Bill of Rights against state interference.

interest group. A group of people that is organized to promote the interests of its members.

Judeo-Christian heritage. Beliefs and practices which have their historical roots in Judaism and Christianity.

judicial branch. The branch of government that interprets and applies the laws through a system of courts.

judicial review. The power of the courts to declare laws and actions of the local, state, or national government invalid if the courts decide they violate the Constitution.

laissez faire. An economic theory that government should not interfere in business, industry, or commerce.

law of nature (or natural law). As used by natural rights philosophers, a moral rule discovered by the use of reason which everyone should obey at all times and places.

legislative branch. The branch of government that makes the laws; in the federal government, this is Congress.

legislative supremacy. A system of government, such as was set forth in the early state constitutions, in which most of the power is given to the legislature.

majority rule. Rule by the more than half of the people in a community.

Magna Carta. A document signed by King John of England in 1215 A.D. that guaranteed certain basic rights to the people. Considered the beginning of constitutional government in England.

mixed government. A form of government which is a mixture of monarchy, aristocracy, and democracy.

monarchy. A government in which political power is exercised by a single ruler under the claim of divine or hereditary right.

natural rights philosophy. The idea that people are naturally endowed with certain rights that may not be taken from them, specifically, the rights to life, liberty, and property.

"necessary and proper" clause. The clause in Article I, Section 8, that gives Congress the power to make all laws that are "necessary and proper" to carry out the powers expressly delegated to it by the Constitution.

nobility. A group of persons having titles, usually of a hereditary nature, who compose the aristocracy in a society. In Great Britain, the nobility is represented in the House of Lords.

null and void. Of no legal or binding force; invalid.

original jurisdiction. The legal authority of a court to be the first to hear a case.

Parliament. The English legislature, made up of two houses, the House of Lords and the House of Commons.

political philosophy. The study of ideas about government and politics.

politics. The activities which concern getting and holding public office and the making of laws.

popular sovereignty. The idea that government is based upon the consent of the people.

private domain. Areas of an individual's life that are not subject to governmental control.

proportional representation. A system in which the number of representatives of a state in the House of Representatives is based on the number of people who live in that state.

procedural due process. Refers to those clauses in the Constitution that protect individuals from unreasonable and unfair governmental procedures.

ratification. Formal approval of the Constitution by the states.

representative democracy. A form of government in which power is held by the people and exercised indirectly through elected representatives.

republic. A form of government in which the supreme political power resides in the people, and administration is exercised by officers elected by the people to represent their interests.

republican government. A system of government in which power is held by the voters and is exercised by elected representatives who are responsible for promoting the common welfare.

royalty. The term refers to the king or other royal persons. It can also mean that part of the government that represents the monarch.

sedition. Language or behavior which seeks to convince others to engage in the overthrow of the government.

"separate but equal". The argument, once upheld by the Supreme Court, that separate public facilities for blacks and whites were constitutional if the facilities were of equal quality.

separation of powers. The division of powers among different branches of government; in the United States, among a legislative, executive, and judicial branch.

social contract. A hypothetical agreement among all the people in a society to give up part of their freedom to a government in return for protection of their natural rights. A theory developed by Locke to explain the origin of government.

sovereign. A person or body of persons in whom the supreme power of the state is vested.

sovereignty. The ultimate, supreme power in a state.

state of nature. The hypothetical condition of people before they lived together in a society with government and laws.

substantive due process. Those judicial interpretations of the due process clauses of the Constitution that require that the content of laws be fair and reasonable.

suffrage. The right to vote.

supremacy clause. Article VI, Section 2, of the Constitution, which states that the Constitution, laws passed by Congress, and treaties of the United States "shall be the supreme law of the land," binding on the states.

three-fifths clause. A clause in the Constitution, now no longer in effect, that provided that each slave should be counted as three-fifths of a person in determining the number of representatives of a state in the House of Representatives and in the collection of direct taxes by Congress.

unalienable (inalienable) rights. Fundamental rights of the people that may not be taken away. A phrase used in the Declaration of Independence.

unitary system. A centralized form of government in which states or local governments exercise only those powers delegated to them by the central or national government.

veto. The constitutional power of the President to refuse to sign a bill passed by Congress.

writ of mandamus. A court order to a government official to perform a specified act. Mandamus is a Latin term meaning "we command."

Biographical Notes

Adams, Abigail. (1744-1818) Wife of President John Adams. Supported her husband in the revolutionary cause. Well known for her letters which have been a rich source of social history.

Adams, John. (1735-1826) Second President of the United States. Lawyer, revolutionary leader, and leading Federalist. As a member of the Continental Congress, he served on the committee to draft the Declaration of Independence. Minister to the Netherlands and Great Britain. Elected Vice President in 1789 and President in 1796.

Anthony, Susan B. (1820-1906) Social reformer involved in both the abolitionist and women suffrage movements. President of National American Woman Suffrage Association. Wrote and lectured in both the United States and Europe for women's suffrage.

Black, Hugo. (1886-1971) Supreme Court Justice from 1937 to 1971. Served in the Senate and was appointed to the Supreme Court by President Roosevelt.

Burger, Warren E. (1907-) Chief Justice of the Supreme Court from 1969 to 1986. Appointed by President Nixon. Named as assistant attorney general in 1953; three years later was appointed to U.S. Court of Appeals for the District of Columbia. Retired in 1986 to head the Commission on the Bicentennial of the United States Constitution.

Burr, Aaron. (1756-1836) Public official and political leader. Served in Continental Army, New York Assembly, and U.S. Senate. Elected as vice president in 1800.

Charles I. (1600-1649) King of England. Believed in the divine right of kings and absolute power of the monarch. Clashed with the House of Commons and ruled seven years without Parliament. Struggle with Parliament led to Civil War and his execution for high treason.

Charles II. (1630-1685) King of England. Son of Charles I, he restored the monarchy in 1660 but continued to have problems with Parliament. Last of the Stuart kings, he was succeeded by his niece, Mary, and her husband, William.

Clinton, George. (1739-1812) Revolutionary soldier and public official. Member of the Continental Congress, governor of New York, general in the Continental Army. Had a profound distrust of centralized government and opposed ratification of the Constitution. Supporter of Jefferson, he served as Vice President in 1804 and 1808.

Cromwell, Oliver. (1599-1658) Lord Protector of England, 1653-1658. Puritan. Military leader in the English Civil War, he upheld the Parliamentary cause and led the army to victory. He united the kingdom, dissolved Parliament, and established himself as ruler until his death.

Dawes, William. (1745-1799) Tradesman, active in the Revolutionary movement in Boston. Gave the warning, with Paul Revere, before the battles of Lexington and Concord. Joined the Continental Army.

Dickinson, John. (1732-1808) Colonial leader. Trained in law, he entered politics in both Pennsylvania and Delaware. As a member of the Continental Congress, he led the committee that wrote the Articles of Confederation. President of the Annapolis Convention and delegate to the Philadelphia Convention. Supported ratification of the Constitution.

Douglas, William. (1898-1980) Supreme Court Justice from 1939 to 1975. Appointed to the Supreme Court by President Franklin D. Roosevelt.

Dyer, Mary. (? -1660) Religious martyr. Born in England and came to Boston in 1635. As a Quaker who preached ideas unpopular with the Puritan leaders of Boston, she was banned from that city under threat of death. When she returned, she was arrested and hanged publicly on June 1, 1660.

Eisenhower, Dwight. (1890-1969) Thirty-fourth President and war hero. Commander of U.S. Forces in Europe during World War II and then elevated to Allied Commander-in-Chief. Elected President in 1954 and reelected four years later. In 1958, ordered federal troops into Little Rock to enforce integration order.

Ellsworth, Oliver. (1745-1807) Chief Justice of the Supreme Court from 1796 to 1800. Active in the Philadelphia Convention, he was an author of the Connecticut Compromise. In 1789, he was elected to the Senate. Responsible for the Judiciary Act of 1789.

Franklin, Benjamin. (1706-1790) Printer, author, inventor, scientist, diplomat, public official. Postmaster of Philadelphia, representative of colonial interests in Great Britain, and member of the Continental Congress. Served on the committee to draft the Declaration of Independence. Served as delegate to the Philadelphia Convention and as America's first ambassador to France.

Gerry, Elbridge. (1744-1814) Vice President of the United States. Member of the Continental Congress and of the Congress of the United States. Federalist. Elected Vice President in 1812.

Hamilton, Alexander. (1755-1804) Federalist leader. Supporter of the revolutionary cause, he served with distinction in the Continental Army. Member of the Continental Congress and the Annapolis Convention. Strong supporter of centralized government, he was a delegate to the Philadelphia Convention but left in frustration. He was one of the authors of *The Federalist*. Served as Secretary of the Treasury under Washington.

Harlan, John Marshall. (1899-1971) Justice of the Supreme Court from 1955 to 1971. Appointed by President Eisenhower.

Harold, King of England. (1022?-1066) Elected on January 6, 1066. Defeated by William, Duke of Normandy, at the Battle of Hastings on October 14, 1066.

Henry, Patrick. (1736-1799) Political leader. Supporter of the revolutionary cause. Opposed the Philadelphia Convention and refused to attend. Led opposition in Virginia to ratification of the Constitution. Worked to include the Bill of Rights in the Constitution.

Henry III. (1207-1272). King of England from 1216 to 1272. Provoked rebellion of nobles who forced him to accept a series of reforms, an important step toward constitutional monarchy. During King Henry's reign, Commons became part of Parliament.

Holmes, Oliver Wendell, Jr. (1841-1935) Justice of the Supreme Court from 1902 to 1932. Appointed by President Theodore Roosevelt. Served 19 years on the Massachusetts Supreme Court.

Hooker, Thomas. (1586-1647) Religious leader. Puritan. Born and educated in England, he fled to Holland and then to Massachusetts. In 1636, he led a group of followers to Connecticut to enjoy religious freedom.

Jackson, Andrew. (1767-1845) Seventh President of the United States. General and hero of the War of 1812. Served in the House and Senate. Came from frontier origins and was seen as representative of the growing democratic spirit in the South and West. Elected President in 1828 and reelected in 1832.

James I. (1566-1625) King of Scotland and England. Son of Mary, Queen of Scots. Sought to assert the divine right of kings.

James II. (1633-1701) King of England, Scotland and Ireland. Son of King Charles I. Favored Roman Catholics and, as a result, was forced to flee to France. English nobles offered the throne to his son-in-law, William of Orange.

Jay, John. (1745-1829) First Chief Justice of the Supreme Court from 1789 to 1795. Wrote New York's first constitution. President of the Continental Congress. Served as minister to Spain and England. Strong supporter of the Constitution and one of the authors of *The Federalist*. Appointed Chief Justice by President Washington but resigned in 1795 when he was elected governor of New York.

Jefferson, Thomas. (1743-1826) Third President of the United States, scientist, philosopher, diplomat, and architect. Supporter of the revolutionary cause. Governor of Virginia. Wrote Declaration of Independence. Supporter of the Constitution but critical of the lack of a bill of rights. First Secretary of State in Washington's cabinet. Leader of the Republican Party. Elected Vice President in 1796 and was chosen President four years later. Reelected to the presidency in 1804.

John, King of England. (1167?-1216) Forced by the nobles to sign the Magna Carta.

Johnson, Lyndon B. (1908-1973) Thirty-sixth President of the United States. Served in both the House and the Senate. Elected in 1955 as Senate Majority Leader. Elected Vice President in 1960. Succeeded to presidency in 1963 upon the assassination of President Kennedy. Elected President in 1964.

Kennedy, John F. (1917-1963) Thirty-fifth President of the United States. Elected to the House of Representatives in 1946; six years later, was elected to the Senate. In 1960, Kennedy became the youngest man and first Catholic ever elected President. Assassinated in 1963.

King, Martin Luther, Jr. (1929-1968) Religious leader and social reformer. Major leader of the civil rights movement in the 1960s, he was an advocate of non-violence. Formed the Southern Christian Leadership Conference in 1957 and became its president. Won the Nobel Peace Prize in 1964. Assassinated in 1968.

Knox, Henry. (1750-1806) Revolutionary military leader. General in the Continental Army and trusted adviser to Washington. Elected Secretary of War under the Articles of Confederation and retained by Washington in that position under the new government.

Locke, John. (1632-1704) English philosopher. Wrote *Two Treatises on Government, Letters Concerning Toleration,* and *An Essay Concerning Human Understanding.* Had a great influence on American political thinkers during the Revolutionary period and the early years of the new nation.

Madison, James. (1751-1836) Fourth President of the United States. Fought for religious freedom in the Virginia constitutional convention. Played a key role at the Philadelphia Convention, offering the Virginia Plan and keeping the only complete record of the debates. One of the authors of *The Federalist.* Played an important role in adding the Bill of Rights to the Constitution. Served as Secretary of State under Jefferson. Elected President in 1808 and reelected in 1812.

Marshall, John. (1755-1835) Chief Justice of the Supreme Court from 1801 to 1835. Supported ratification of the Constitution and led Federalist Party in Virginia. Member of the House of Representatives. Served 34 years as Chief Justice, interpreting the Constitution in a manner that reflected his belief in a strong and effective national government.

Marshall, Thurgood. (1908-   ) Justice of the Supreme Court, appointed in 1967 by President Johnson. Great-grandson of slaves, he became involved in the civil rights movement. As counsel for the NAACP, he successfully pleaded the case of *Brown v. Board of Education* in 1954. First black judge to serve on the Supreme Court.

Martin, Luther. (1748?-1826) Lawyer and supporter of the revolutionary cause. As a delegate to the Philadelphia Convention, he opposed a strong central government. Walked out of the Convention and fought ratification.

Mason, George. (1725-1792) Political leader. Drafted Virginia's first constitution and bill of rights. Member of the Virginia House of Delegates. Attended Philadelphia Convention but opposed a strong central government. Left the Philadelphia Convention and fought ratification of the Constitution.

Montesquieu. (1689-1755) French lawyer, author, political philosopher. Wrote the *Spirit of the Laws* (1748) which greatly influenced political thought in Europe and America. Formulated doctrine of separation of powers in government.

Morris, Gouverneur. (1752-1816) Public leader, diplomat, and lawyer. Member of the Continental Congress and delegate to the Philadelphia Convention. Advocate of a strong national government. Principally responsible for final literary form of the Constitution.

Paine, Thomas. (1737-1809) Author and political theorist. Born in England, he came to America in November, 1774. In early 1776, he published the pamphlet *Common Sense* which stirred many Americans to the revolutionary cause. During the war, his pamphlets, *The Crisis*, helped support the Revolution and encouraged the soldiers in the Continental Army.

Randolph, Edmund. (1753-1813) Public official and lawyer. Delegate to the Continental Congress, the Annapolis Convention, and the Philadelphia Convention. Served on the committee that drafted the final form of the Constitution, but refused to sign because he thought it gave too much power to the president. By the time of the Virginia convention, he urged ratification. Served as the first attorney general under the new government and then succeeded Jefferson as secretary of state.

Revere, Paul. (1735-1818) Silversmith and revolutionary patriot. Leader of the Boston Sons of Liberty. Principal express rider for the Boston Committee of Safety, spreading news of revolutionary activities, including his famous ride of April 18, 1775, warning of the forthcoming attack of British troops.

Rutledge, John. (1739-1800) Justice of the Supreme Court from 1789 to 1791. Appointed by President Washington. Delegate to the Stamp Act Congress, the Continental Congress, and the Philadelphia Convention. Helped write South Carolina's first constitution and served as governor of that state.

Shays, Daniel. (1747?-1825) Revolutionary soldier and postwar rebel. One of several leaders of the revolt in western Massachusetts against the state government. In 1786, he led armed farmers in a raid on the Springfield arsenal. Fled to Vermont when his band was defeated and later settled in New York.

Sherman, Roger. (1721-1793) Lawyer and public official. Delegate to the Continental Congress, he signed the Declaration of Independence. One of the drafters of the Articles of Confederation. Delegate from Connecticut to the Philadelphia Convention. Served in U.S. House of Representatives and Senate.

Socrates. (470?-399 BC) Greek philosopher. Used an original question-and-answer method of instruction with his pupils, the most famous of whom was Plato. Drank poison in prison rather than give up his teaching when authorities ordered him to do.

Thoreau, Henry David. (1817-1862) Naturalist, philosopher, author. Lived for two years at Walden Pond to demonstrate the simple, self-reliant life. In 1849, he published his essay "On the Duty of Civil Disobedience." Was imprisoned for one day in 1846 for refusing to pay a tax supporting the Mexican War which he opposed.

Truman, Harry. (1884-1972) Thirty-third President of the United States. Elected to the Senate from Missouri in 1934. Chosen as Franklin Roosevelt's running mate in 1944, he succeeded to the presidency upon Roosevelt's death in April, 1945, and was reelected in 1948.

Warren, Earl. (1891-1974) Chief Justice of the Supreme Court from 1953 to 1969. Appointed by President Eisenhower. Was attorney general and governor of California. In 1954, he announced the landmark decision in *Brown v. Board of Education.*

Warren, Mercy Otis. (1728-1814) Author. Anti-Federalist. Knew most of the Revolutionary leaders personally and spent much of her life at the center of events. Her vantage point, combined with her literary talents, made her a well-known historian and poet. Wrote several plays and a three-volume history of the Revolution.

Washington, George. (1732-1799) First President, military hero, planter, Revolutionary leader. Commander-in-chief of the Continental Army during the Revolution. Delegate to the Philadelphia Convention where he was unanimously chosen as president. Agreed reluctantly to become the first President of the United States. Retired after two terms in office.

William the Conqueror. (1027-1087) First Norman king in England. Introduced the feudal order to the old Anglo-Saxon system of government.

Wilson, James. (1742-1798) Justice of the Supreme Court from 1789 to 1798. Appointed by President Washington. Lawyer in Pennsylvania, he served in the Continental Congress, and signed the Declaration of Independence. Played a key role at the Philadelphia Convention. Wrote the Pennsylvania state constitution.

Yates, Robert. (1738-1801) Revolutionary patriot, jurist, and Anti-Federalist leader. Delegate to the Philadelphia Convention, he left because he felt that the Convention exceeded its authority in writing a new constitution. Served on New York Supreme Court and was chief justice of that court from 1790-1798.

Zenger, John Peter. (1697-1746) Printer and editor. Served as editor of an anti-government newspaper and, in 1733, was arrested for seditious libel. His defense was handled by Andrew Hamilton who urged jury to consider the truth of Zenger's statements. The jury did so, Zenger was acquitted, and his name became linked with freedom of the press.

Important Dates

509-27 B.C.	Roman Republic		1787-1788	Publication of *The Federalist*
1066 A.D.	Battle of Hastings		1788	Ratification of the Constitution
1215	Magna Carta		1789	First Congress
1258	Establishment of Parliament		1789	Washington elected president
1607	First English settlement in America		1789	Judiciary Act
1619	First colonial legislative assembly		1791	Ratification of the Bill of Rights
1620	Pilgrims settle at Plymouth		1791	First Bank of the United States
1628	English Petition of Right		1796	Adams elected president
1649	Execution of Charles I		1798	Alien and Sedition Acts
1653-1660	Protectorate rules England		1798	Virginia and Kentucky Resolutions
1660	English monarchy restored		1800	Jefferson elected president
1689	English Bill of Rights		1803	*Marbury v. Madison*
1689	English Toleration Act		1816	Second Bank of the United States
1754-1763	French-Indian War		1819	*McCulloch v. Maryland*
1765	Stamp Act and Quartering Act		1846-1848	War with Mexico
1767	Townshend Acts		1848	First women's rights convention
1770	Boston Massacre		1861-1865	Civil War
1773	Tea Act and Boston Tea Party		1865	Ratification of the 13th Amendment
1774	Intolerable Acts		1868	Ratification of the 14th Amendment
1774	First Continental Congress		1870	Ratification of the 15th Amendment
1775	Battles of Lexington and Concord		1890	National American Woman Suffrage Assn.
1775	Second Continental Congress		1896	*Plessy v. Ferguson*
1776	Declaration of Independence		1920	Ratification of the 19th Amendment
1780	Massachusetts state constitution		1954	*Brown v. Board of Eduction*
1781	Ratification of the Articles of Confederation		1964	Civil Rights Act
1786	Shays' Rebellion		1965	Voting Rights Act
1786	Annapolis Convention		1968	Equal Employment Opportunities Act
1787	Philadelphia Convention		1971	Ratification of the 26th Amendment

Index of Supreme Court Cases

Index